Grades **3-6**

Scott Foresman

Phonics and Decoding
Teacher's Guide and Student Worktext

Glenview, Illinois
Boston, Massachusetts
Chandler, Arizona
Upper Saddle River, New Jersey

ISBN-13: 978-0-328-47781-4
ISBN-10:   0-328-47781-8
8 9 10 V016 18 17 16 15 14 13

Reading Street Response to Intervention Kit

Program Overview

The *Reading Street Response to Intervention Kit* provides targeted instruction in core English-Language Arts standards for Grades 3 to 6 in each of the five critical areas of reading instruction: phonemic awareness, phonics and decoding, fluency, vocabulary, and comprehension. The Kit, designed for small-group or one-on-one instruction, includes lessons on core skills, allowing teachers to focus on the skills students need most and help them make rapid progress to achieve grade-level proficiency. For additional information about the *Reading Street Response to Intervention Kit*, see "How to Use This Kit" in the RTI Kit Implementation Guide.

Phonics Teacher's Guide and Student Worktext

The Teacher's Guide portion includes
- three-tiered, differentiated lessons for 30 phonics and decoding topics
- mini-lessons on specific symbol-sound relationships, spelling patterns, phonograms, letter combinations, and other elements of phonics and decoding
- reinforcement for the strategies and routines used in the core program
- word lists to practice and reinforce each phonics and decoding topic

The Student Worktext portion includes
- additional practice
- word cards and other manipulatives
- School+Home activities on every page

Lesson Features
- **Set the scene** introduces the lesson topic to students.
- **Objectives** identify the instructional objectives for students.
- **Materials** list the Worktext components and additional supporting materials for the lesson, such as the Routine Cards.
- **Direct teaching** is provided through explicit teacher modeling and consistent routines.
- **Mini-lessons** are provided for differentiated instruction.
- **Guided practice** for each mini-lesson consists of ample group practice with multiple response opportunities.
- **Independent practice (On Their Own)** allows students to practice with teacher guidance.
- **If…/then…** provides teachers with specific activities for reinforcing skills.

Table of Contents Phonics and Decoding

Phonics and Decoding Teacher's Guide

Common Letter-Sound Correspondences

This lesson demonstrates the instruction you will use for Word Lists 1–26.

Objective:
• Teach all consonant and short vowel sounds.

MATERIALS
• Worktext
  p. 2 (Word Lists 1–9),
  p. 3 (Word Lists 10–18),
  p. 4 (Word Lists 19–26)
• Routine Card 1

Set the scene Remind students that letters are used to spell sounds. Today we are going to learn about the sound /m/ and its spelling.

Routine

1 Teach the Letters Write the letters *Mm*. The name for these letters is *m*. Point to *M*. The name of this letter is capital (uppercase) *M*. What is the name of this letter? Repeat with lowercase *m*. Tell students that *m* is a consonant. A consonant is any letter of the alphabet that is not a vowel. Model writing the letters *M* and *m* and have students write them.

2 Connect Sound to Spelling Display a picture of something that begins with the letter *m*, such as the moon. What is this a picture of? What sound do you hear at the beginning of the word *moon*? (/m/) Have students say /m/ several times as you point to *m*.

3 Model and Give Examples Now we're going to write the letter *m* to spell the sound /m/. Tell students that you will say a word, and they should listen to its beginning sound. If the word begins with /m/, we'll write the letter *m*. Say *monkey*, emphasizing the beginning sound. What's the first sound in *monkey*? (/m/) Write the letter *m*. Then say a distracter, such as *baseball*. Do you hear /m/? (no) Repeat the procedure with a word that ends in *m*, such as *slam*.

Model blending a word such as *mop* as students become familiar with short vowels. We're going to use sounds and letters we know to read words. Write *m* and say /m/. Add *o* and say /o/. Blend *mo*: /m//o/. Add *p* and say /p/. Run your hand under *mop* as you blend the word.

4 Guide Practice Use the first five words in the Word List to continue the activity in step 3. This time have students identify the beginning sound. As students become familiar with short vowels, have them blend the words with you using Routine Card 1.

5 Practice and Review Provide practice writing the letter *m* for /m/ by using the Word List. Say a word from each column one at a time, and have students identify whether each word begins or ends with /m/. If students are able, display the words and have students blend them. To review Word Lists 1–9, see Worktext p. 2. To review Word Lists 10–18, see p. 3. To review Word Lists 19–26, see p. 4.

Word Lists 1–9

Begin with the initial list. As students progress, continue with the final and medial lists. To review Word Lists 1–9, see Worktext p. 2.

Word List 1 (*Mm*, /m/ *m*)

Initial	Final	Medial
mug	am	lemon
made	drum	number
mail	from	bumpy
March	bottom	family
Monday	plum	camel

Word List 2 (*Ss*, /s/ *s*, *ss*)

Initial	Final	Medial
sip	gas	also
sun	yes	closer
Saturday	atlas	lesson*
soccer	dress*	bison
sorry	mess*	basket

*Use these words to point out that the /s/ sound can also be spelled *ss*.

Word List 3 (*Tt*, /t/ *t*, *tt*)

Initial	Final	Medial
ten	set	attic*
tub	flat	bottle*
Tuesday	cut	lettuce*
telephone	lit	button*
today	bat	kitten*

*Point out that /t/ can also be spelled *tt*.

Word List 4 (*Aa*, /a/ *a*)

Initial	Medial
am	back
an	hand
at	happy
apple	lamp
ant	wagon
add	clap

Word List 5 (*Cc*, /k/ *c*, *ck*)

Initial	Final	Medial
call	Mac	pocket*
cover	brick*	rocket*
camera	check*	socket*
corn	pack*	
catch	truck*	

*Point out that /k/ can also be spelled *ck*.

Word List 6 (*Pp*, /p/ *p*, *pp*)

Initial	Final	Medial
pat	cup	apart
pear	stop	paper
plant	ship	upon
penny	dip	happen*
pickle	chop	apple*

*Point out that /p/ can also be spelled *pp*.

Word List 7 (*Nn*, /n/ *n*)

Initial	Final	Medial
net	fun	final
never	even	banjo
nickel	green	money
nurse	train	until
neck	ten	animal

Word List 8 (*Ii*, /i/ *i*)

Initial	Medial
it	city
ink	dig
in	finish
if	gift
into	stick

Word List 9 (*Ff*, /f/ *f*, *ff*)

Initial	Final	Medial
fit	if	safety
farm	roof	wafer
fast	beef	muffin*
father	off*	traffic*
fin	stuff*	waffle*

*Point out that /f/ can also be spelled *ff*.

Word Lists 10–18

Begin with the initial list. As students progress, continue with the final and medial lists. To review Word Lists 10–18, see Worktext p. 3.

Word List 10 (*Bb, /b/ b*)

Initial	Final	Medial
bit	crab	about
bad	tab	cabin
bumpy	grab	number
balloon	rib	robot
busy	web	habit

Word List 11 (*Gg, /g/ g, gg*)

Initial	Final	Medial
got	bag	ago
game	frog	again
garden	jog	begin
gift	rug	juggle*
good	wag	wiggle*

*Point out that /g/ can also be spelled *gg*.

Word List 12 (*Oo, /o/ o*)

Initial	Medial
odd	top
olive	body
option	drop
ox	plot
otter	sock

Word List 13 (*Dd, /d/ d*)

Initial	Final	Medial
dip	sad	body
dime	food	idea
down	loud	spider
deer	toad	study
duck	sled	wonder

Word List 14 (*Ll, /l/ l, ll*)

Initial	Final	Medial
look	April	always
lamb	nail	belong
lemon	pencil	elbow
lion	small*	follow*
lunch	will*	gallon*

*Point out that /l/ can also be spelled *ll*.

Word List 15 (*Hh, /h/ h*)

Initial	
hat	head
has	help
he	here
her	hippo
hen	hurry

Word List 16 (*Ee, /e/ e*)

Initial	Medial
egg	bell
edge	best
enter	clever
enjoy	sled
ever	vest

Word List 17 (*Rr, /r/ r, rr*)

Initial	Final	Medial
race	bear	cart
ride	door	berry*
radio	ever	mirror*
road	number	parrot*
round	your	sorry*

*Point out that /r/ can also be spelled *rr*.

Word List 18 (*Ww, /w/ w*)

Initial		Medial
win	want	always
was	watch	homework
week	woman	awake
warm	would	highway
web	wolf	away

Word Lists 19–26

Begin with the initial list. As students progress, continue with the final and medial lists. To review Word Lists 19–26, see Worktext p. 4.

Word List 19 (*Jj*, /j/ *j*)

Initial

jam	January
jab	juice
jet	July
jeep	jump
joke	jungle

Word List 20 (*Kk*, /k/ *k*)

Initial	**Final**	**Medial**
kid	cook	baker
key	break	broken
kept	duck*	taken
kind	speak	worker
kitten	pick*	basket

*Point out that /k/ can also be spelled *ck*.

Word List 21 (*Uu*, /u/ *u*)

Initial	**Medial**
up	cup
us	drum
under	funny
until	study
upon	puzzle

Word List 22 (*Vv*, /v/ *v*)

Initial	**Final**	**Medial**
vet	Bev	never
vase	Liv	seven
very	Lev	river
violin		clever
volcano		shovel

Word List 23 (*Yy*, /y/ *y*)

Initial

yell	yawn
yum	yard
yap	young
yes	yellow
yet	yank

Word List 24 (*Zz*, /z/ *z, zz*)

Initial	**Final**	**Medial**
zip	fuzz*	puzzle*
zero	jazz*	fuzzy*
zone	whiz	drizzle*
zipper	fizz*	blizzard*
zebra	Liz	nuzzle*

*Point out that /z/ can also be spelled *zz*.

Word List 25 (*Qq*, /kw/ *qu*)

Initial

quit	question
quiet	quick
quiz	quart
queen	quarter
quilt	quack

Word List 26 (*Xx*, /ks/ *x*)

Final

ox	six
ax	box
pox	wax
Max	fox
fix	mix

Phonics and Decoding Lesson 2
Initial Blends and Three-Letter Blends

Objectives:
- Teach concept of initial consonant blends.
- Introduce initial *l* and *r* blends.
- Introduce initial *s* blends.
- Introduce three-letter initial blends with *s.*

MATERIALS
- Worktext pp. 5–7
- Routine Cards 1, 2
- Letter tiles

Set the scene Remind students that words are made up of sounds and that we write vowels and consonants to spell the sounds. In this lesson, you will learn to read and spell words that blend the sounds of *l, r,* and *s* with other consonants.

Routine **1. Connect Sound to Spelling** Connect today's lesson to previously learned sound-spellings. Write *lap* and *rat.* Say each word, emphasizing the initial sound. Be sure students can identify the initial sound of *lap* as /l/ and the initial sound of *rat* as /r/. Today you'll learn to spell and read words that combine these sounds with other letter sounds you know.

2. Model and Give Examples Write and say *plan.* Point to the first two letters. The sound /p/ can be combined with the sound /l/. When the sounds are blended together, you can still hear the sounds of both letters. Say /p//l/. Have students repeat the sound several times with you. Then write *drip* and repeat the procedure to introduce the initial *dr* blend.

3. Model Blending Explain that now students will use sounds and letters they know to read whole words. Write *cl* and say /k//l/. Add *a* and say /a/. Run your hand under the letters as you say /k//l//a/. Add *p* and say /p/. The run your hand under *clap* as you model blending the whole word: /k//l//a//p/. Have students repeat *clap* several times. Follow this procedure to help students read *drill,* which has an initial *r* blend. Discuss the meaning of these words with students and help them use each one in a sentence.

Mini-Lesson 1 Initial *l* and *r* Blends

Remind students that...
- Blends contain two or more consecutive consonants, each of which is pronounced and blended with the other, as *fl* in *flag.*
- Many words contain initial *l* and *r* blends.

Word List

blot	brim
club	crab
flip	grill
glad	proud
plain	track

Guide Practice
Write and point to *blob.* Use step 3 of the routine above to model sound-by-sound blending. Have students blend *blob* with and without you: /b//l//o//b/. Follow the procedure with the *cl, fl, gl, pl,* and *sl* blends in the words below. Use the words in sentences and discuss each one's meaning.

blob	cliff	floss	glass	plus	slam

Repeat the process with *br, cr, fr, gr, pr,* and *tr* blends in the words below.

bright	crack	from	grin	prop	trot

If... students cannot read a word,
then... say each sound as you point to the letter or letters that spell that sound (Routine Card 1). Have students blend the sounds without stopping between them.

On Their Own For additional practice, use the Word List and Worktext p. 5. Help students spell each word with letter tiles.

Mini-Lesson 2 — Initial *s* Blends

Remind students that...
- Blends contain two or more consecutive consonants, each of which is pronounced and blended with the other, as *fl* in *flag*.
- Many words begin with initial *s* blends.

Word List

scared	spell
skid	stay
smack	swing
snail	

Guide Practice

Use sound-by-sound blending strategies (Routine Cards 1, 2) to help students read words with initial *s* blends *sc, sk, sm,* and *sn.* Write them and ask students to identify each letter. Then point to each letter combination. What are the blended sounds for this letter combination? Have students repeat each blend with you. Then write the words below. Run your hand under the letters in each word as you blend the whole word. Follow this procedure to help students read each word. Discuss word meanings together.

scab   skit   smog   snug

Repeat the process with *sp, st,* and *sw* blends in the words below.

spend   start   stool   swim

If... students cannot read a word,
then... point to the initial two letters and have students practice blending the sounds. Run your hand under the rest of the word as you read it.

On Their Own See Worktext p. 6 and the Word List for additional practice. Take turns using each word in a sentence.

Mini-Lesson 3 — Three-Letter *s* Blends

Remind students that...
- Blends contain two or more consecutive consonants, each of which is pronounced and blended with the other, as *fl* in *flag*.
- Many words start with three-letter blends beginning with *s.*

Word List

scrape	squeak
splat	string
spray	

Guide Practice

Write the five words below. What do you notice about the beginning sounds in these words? Explain that in this lesson students will learn several three-letter blends beginning with the letter *s: scr, spl, spr, squ,* and *str.* Circle the first three letters in *scream.* These letters spell the sounds /s//k//r/ as in the word *scream.* Run your hand under *scream* as you model blending the word: /s//k//r//ē//m/. Have students blend with you. Follow this procedure to model the remaining words below. Use each word in a sentence to help students understand the words' meanings.

scream   split   sprain   squeeze   stroke

If... students have difficulty reading a word,
then... remind them to blend the sounds of the first three letters. Encourage them to say the sounds in their heads before reading the word aloud.

On Their Own For additional practice, use Worktext p. 7 and the Word List. After students can read each word, use it in a sentence and ask what it means.

Phonics and Decoding Lesson 3
Final Blends

Objectives:

- Teach concept of final consonant blends.
- Introduce final *nd, nt, mp,* and *ft* blends.
- Introduce final *lt, ld, lp,* and *lf* blends.
- Introduce final *sk, sp,* and *st* blends.

MATERIALS

- Worktext pp. 8–10
- Routine Cards 1, 2
- Letter tiles

Set the scene Remind students that, when two consonants appear next to each other, the sounds may be blended together. You learned how to blend sounds that come at the beginning of a word. Today we will learn how to read words that end with two consonant sounds blended closely together.

Routine

1. Connect Sound to Spelling Write and say *flip* and *crime.* Ask students what they notice about the first sounds in these words. (The words begin with two consonant sounds blended together.) In this lesson you'll learn to blend words with final consonant sounds.

2. Model and Give Examples Write this sentence: *I will hunt for the band music.* Underline *hunt.* Point to *nt.* When you see two consonants at the end of a word, try blending the sounds closely together. What sounds do you hear at the end of *hunt?* Have students repeat the sound /n//t/ several times. Ask them to find another word in the sentence that ends with two consonants (*band*). Have them practice blending the sound /n//d/.

3. Model Blending Run your hand under *hunt.* Say each sound by itself: /h//u//n//t/, *hunt.* Have students blend the sounds with and without you. Repeat the process to model reading *band.* Remind students that to say the word, they should say all the sounds in the word quickly. Then ask students to explain the meaning of each word. Challenge students to think of another meaning of *band* (for example, a rubber band, a watch band, or a wedding band). Look for words that end with two sounds blended closely together as you read.

Mini-Lesson 1 Final Blends *nd, nt, mp, ft*

Remind students that...

- Blends contain two or more consecutive consonants, each of which is pronounced and blended with the other, as *nd* in *land.*
- Consonant sounds may be blended together at the end of a word.
- The final blends *nd, nt, mp,* and *ft* are used in many words.

Word List

blend	rent	camp	raft
find	spent	lamp	left

Guide Practice

Help students practice saying and reading words that end with **nd, nt, mp,** and **ft** by repeating steps 2 and 3 of the routine above. Focus first on *nd* and *nt* blends. Write each word and circle the final letter combination. Ask for its sounds. Model blending the whole word and then ask

students to blend with you. Discuss the meaning of each word with students and help them use each word in a sentence.

blind	wand	mint	plant

Continue the procedure with the *mp* and *ft* final blends in the words below.

stamp	thump	craft	draft

If... students cannot read a word,

then... circle the final blend and have students say the sounds as you touch under the last two letters. Model blending each sound-spelling to say the word (Routine Cards 1 and 2).

On Their Own For additional practice, use Worktext p. 8 and the Word List. Help students use letter tiles to spell and read each word on the list.

Mini-Lesson 2 — Final Blends *lt, ld, lp, lf*

Remind students that...
- Blends contain two or more consecutive consonants, each of which is pronounced and closely blended with the other, as *nd* in *land.*
- Consonant blends may come at the end of a word.
- The final blends *lt, ld, lp,* and *lf* are used in many words.

Word List
quilt	build	gulp	elf
melt	child	pulp	wolf

Guide Practice
Use the routine to blend final consonant sounds *lt, ld, lp,* and *lf.* Write *halt* and *knelt.* What do you notice about how these words end? Point to *lt.* When the /l/ and the /t/ sounds are combined, the sounds are blended together: /l//t/. Run your hand under the letters as you read each word: /h//ȯ//l//t/, *halt*; /n//e//l//t/, *knelt.* Have students read the words aloud several times. Follow this procedure to help students read the remaining words below. After students can read the words, discuss their meanings.

halt	knelt	bald	shield	scalp	golf

If... students have difficulty blending sounds,
then... have them say the sounds in their heads before reading the word aloud. Slowly blend the whole word and ask students to repeat the sounds after you.

On Their Own See Worktext p. 9 and the Word List for additional practice. Monitor students as they read each word and have them use each word in a sentence.

Mini-Lesson 3 — Final Blends *sk, sp, st*

Remind students that...
- Blends contain two or more consecutive consonants, each of which is pronounced and closely blended with the other, as *nd* in *land.*
- Consonant blends may come at the end of a word.
- The final blends *sk, sp,* and *st* are used in many words.

Word List
mask	clasp	trust
risk	gasp	wrist

Guide Practice
Remind students that two consonant sounds are sometimes blended together at the end of a word. Write *brisk* and use it in a sentence: *The brisk wind made me feel cold.* Ask students to identify the two sounds at the end of *brisk* (/s/ and /k/). Run your hand under the letters as you say the whole word: /br//i//s//k/. Follow this procedure to model the *sk, sp,* and *st* blends in the other words below. Then use each word in a sentence and encourage questions about and discussion of the meanings of the words.

brisk	task	grasp	wasp	crust	twist

If... students have difficulty reading the words,
then... have them say the sound as you touch under each sound-spelling. Move your hand from letter to letter as you say the sounds without pausing between them.

On Their Own For additional practice, use Worktext p. 10. Also, have students use letter tiles to build and read the Word List words.

Phonics and Decoding Lesson 4
Consonant Digraphs

Objectives:
- Teach concept of consonant digraphs.
- Introduce /sh/ *sh* digraph.
- Introduce /th/ *th* digraph.
- Introduce /f/ *ph* and /f/ *gh* digraphs.

MATERIALS
- Worktext pp. 11–13
- Routine Cards 1, 2
- Letter tiles

Set the scene Explain that in this lesson students will learn to spell and read words with two consonants that spell one sound. Today we will learn to read words with the sounds /sh/, /th/, and /f/. Each of these sounds may be spelled by two consonants.

Routine

1. Connect Sound to Spelling Connect today's lesson to previously learned sound-spellings. Write *plain* and *camp*. What do you know about the first sounds in *plain* and the last sounds in *camp*? (The two consonant sounds are closely blended together.) Say the words and exaggerate the blended /pl/ and /mp/ sounds. Today we will learn about consonants that work together to stand for one sound.

2. Model and Give Examples Write and say *shed*. Point to the letters *sh*. What is the sound for these letters? Ask students to repeat the first sound in *shed* with you: /sh/. Write *cash*. Ask students what sound they hear at the end of *cash*. When you see *sh* in a word, try /sh/.

3. Model Blending Explain that now students will use sounds and letters they know to read whole words. Write *sh* and say /sh/. Add *e* and say /e/. Run your hand under the letters as you say /sh//e/. Add *d* and say /d/. Then run your hand under *shed* as you model blending the whole word: /sh//e//d/. Have students repeat *shed* several times. Follow this procedure to help students blend *cash*. Discuss the meaning of these words with students. Invite them to use each in a sentence. Encourage them to brainstorm other words that begin or end with the sound /sh/.

Mini-Lesson 1 Consonant Digraph /sh/ *sh*

Remind students that...
- Digraphs are two consecutive letters that stand for a single sound, such as *sh* or *th*.
- Some consonant digraphs may appear at the beginning or end of a word.
- The consonant digraph /sh/ *sh* is used in many words.

Word List

share	brush
shift	mash
shove	squish

Guide Practice
Repeat the routine above to help students read and spell words with /sh/ *sh*. Write *shake* and circle the letters *sh*. What sound do these letters stand for? Say /sh/ with students several times. Then run your hand under *shake* as you blend the sounds: /sh//ā//k/. Repeat the process to introduce the remaining words. Encourage students to discuss each word's meaning and to use it in a sentence.

shake	sharp	shock
crush	flash	trash

If... students cannot read a word,
then... say each sound as you point to the letter or letters that spell that sound (Routine Card 1). Have students blend the sounds without stopping between them.

On Their Own For more practice, use Worktext p. 11. For additional practice, use letter tiles to help students spell and read the words on the Word List. Use each word in a sentence to help students understand its meaning.

Mini-Lesson 2 — Consonant Digraph /th/ *th*

Remind students that...

- Digraphs are two consecutive letters that stand for a single sound, such as *sh* or *th*.
- Some consonant digraphs may appear at the beginning or end of a word.
- The consonant digraph **/th/** *th* is used in many words.

Word List

thank	booth
third	month
think	teeth

Guide Practice

Use sound-by-sound and word-by-word blending strategies (Routine Cards 1, 2) to help students connect **/th/** with *th* and to blend words that begin and end with *th*. Write the first two words below and say them aloud several times. What sound do you hear at the beginning of each word? What two letters spell that sound? Run your

hand under the words as you and students say them: /th//ȯ/, *thaw;* /th//ē//m/, *theme.* Repeat the process with the remaining words. Discuss the words' meanings with students.

thaw	theme	thorn
death	mouth	truth

If... students cannot read a word,

then... write each letter, blend, or digraph and ask for its sound(s). Have students blend the word with and without you.

On Their Own See Worktext p. 12 and the Word List for additional practice with words with /th/. Help students build each word with letter tiles. Remind them to try /th/ for the letters *th.* Work together to use each word in a sentence.

Mini-Lesson 3 — Consonant Digraphs /f/ *ph, gh*

Remind students that...

- Digraphs are two consecutive letters that stand for a single sound, such as *sh* or *th*.
- Some consonant digraphs may appear at the beginning, middle, or end of a word.
- The consonant digraphs **/f/** *ph* and **/f/** *gh* are used in many words.

Word List

phase	graphic
photograph	nephew
cough	elephant
laugh	

Guide Practice

Remind students that sounds can be spelled different ways. Write *fire, leaf, photo,* and *laugh.* Read the words aloud and ask students to repeat. What sound do all three words include? Help students identify the sound /f/ in

the words. Sometimes the sound /f/ is spelled with *f* (point to *fire* and *leaf*). In other words (point to *photo* and *laugh*), the letters *ph* and *gh* can spell /f/. Write each word below. Point to each spelling as you say its sound and have students blend the words with you. Discuss the meanings of the words.

phony	graph	rough
trophy	telephone	

If... students have difficulty reading a word,

then... remind them to try the sound /f/ when they see *ph* or *gh.* Model using sound-by-sound blending (Routine Card 1).

On Their Own For additional practice, use Worktext p. 13 and the Word List. Monitor students as they blend the sounds in each word. Encourage students to use each word in a sentence.

Phonics and Decoding Lesson 5
More Consonant Digraphs

Objectives:
- Teach concept of consonant digraphs.
- Introduce /ch/ *ch, tch* digraphs.
- Introduce /hw/ *wh* digraph.
- Introduce /k/ *ch* and /sh/ *ch* digraphs.

MATERIALS
- Worktext pp. 14–16
- Routine Cards 1, 2
- Letter tiles

Set the scene Remind students that in some words consonants work together to spell one sound. In this lesson, you will learn to spell and read words with the sounds /ch/, /hw/, /k/, and /sh/.

Routine **1. Connect Sound to Spelling** Write *thin* and *phone*. Ask students what they notice about the first sounds in these words. (Both words begin with two consonants that stand for one sound. The sound /th/ is spelled *th*; /f/ is spelled *ph*.) Today you will learn to connect /ch/ with *ch* and *tch* and to read words with these letters.

2. Model and Give Examples Write *chest*. What is the first sound in this word? Point to *ch* and have students say it with you: /ch/. Which letters work together to spell /ch/? Point to the *ch* in *chest*. Follow this procedure to model the final sound in *match*. Explain to students that /ch/ can be spelled *ch* or *tch*.

3. Model Blending Use the sound-by-sound blending strategy to say the whole word. Write *ch* and say /ch/. Add *e* and blend the sounds: /ch//e/. Then add *st*. Run your hand under *chest* as you have students blend the word with you: /ch//e//s//t/. Follow this procedure to model blending *match*. Remind students that the /ch/ sound may come at the beginning or end of a word. Discuss the meaning of *chest* and *match* and have students use each word in a sentence. Encourage students to think of sentences that use each word in different ways (for example, *a treasure chest, a pain in the chest; a tennis match, a match to light a fire*).

Mini-Lesson 1 Consonant Digraphs /ch/ *ch, tch*

Remind students that...
- Consonant digraphs are consecutive consonants that stand for a single sound.
- Some digraphs may appear at the beginning or end of a word.
- The consonant digraphs **/ch/ *ch, tch*** appear in many words.

Word List
chain	bunch	blotch
choke	teach	catch
chug	touch	scratch

Guide Practice
Help students read words with **/ch/** spelled *ch* and *tch* by using the routine above. After you write each word below, circle *ch*. What sound do these letters spell? Say /ch/ aloud several times as you point to *ch*. Remind students that the sound /ch/ may come at the beginning or end of

a word. Blend each word and have students repeat each word after you.

change	**chapter**	**chess**	**branch**	**crunch**

Continue the procedure to introduce /ch/ spelled *tch* in the words below.

clutch	**ditch**	**hatch**	**pitch**	**stretch**

Encourage students to also think about and discuss the word meanings.

If... students cannot read a word,
then... exaggerate /ch/ as you say each word several times. Then point to each sound-spelling as students blend the word without pausing between sounds (Routine Card 1).

On Their Own For additional practice, use Worktext p. 14. Provide more practice with the Word List. Help students use letter tiles to spell and read each word on the list.

Mini-Lesson 2 — Consonant Digraph /hw/ *wh*

Remind students that...
- Consonant digraphs are consecutive consonants that stand for a single sound.
- The consonant digraph **/hw/ *wh*** appears at the beginning of many words.

Word List

where	whine
which	whistle
while	white

Guide Practice

Remind students that they have learned to read words that begin with *w* (such as *win*) and with *h* (such as *hit*). Today you'll learn to spell and read words with **/hw/** spelled *wh*. Write *whack.* Point to *wh.* What sound do these letters spell? Have students say /hw/ several times.

Run your hand under *whack* as you say its sounds: /hw//a//k/. Then have students blend with you. Repeat the procedure to model blending the remaining words below. Be sure that students understand each word's meaning.

whack   wheeze   whiff   whirl   whisper

If... students have difficulty reading a word,
then... have students say the sounds as you touch under the letter or letters (Routine Card 2). Remind students to try the sound /hw/ when they see *wh* together in a word.

On Their Own See Worktext p. 15 and the Word List for additional practice. Help students use letter tiles to spell each word. Then help students think of a sentence that uses each word.

Note: In some dialects *wh* is pronounced /w/ rather than /hw/.

Mini-Lesson 3 — Consonant Digraphs /k/ *ch* and /sh/ *ch*

Remind students that...
- Consonant digraphs are consecutive consonants that stand for a single sound.
- The consonant digraphs **/k/ *ch*** and **/sh/ *ch*** appear in many words.

Word List

chord	brochure
ache	machine
stomach	parachute

Guide Practice

Connect today's lesson to previously learned sound-spellings *c* and *sh*. Write *cat* and *ship*. Remind students that the sound /k/ can be spelled with *c* and that the sound /sh/ can be spelled with *sh*. Today you'll learn to spell and read words with the sounds **/k/** and **/sh/** spelled *ch*. One at a time, write each word below.

Then run your hand under the whole word as you blend its sounds. Have students blend with you. After students can blend each word, discuss its meaning. Invite students to use each word in a sentence.

chrome   anchor   chorus   chef   chute

If... students have difficulty reading a word,
then... point to the letters *ch* and help students decide if *ch* spells the /k/ or /sh/ sound. Have students blend the sounds in the word slowly at first and then more quickly.

On Their Own For additional practice, use the Word List and Worktext p. 16. Help students understand the meaning of any unfamiliar words.

Final Digraphs and Sounds

Objectives:

- Teach concept of final digraphs and sounds.
- Introduce final **/k/ ck.**
- Introduce final **/j/ dge.**
- Introduce final **/ng/ ng** and **/ngk/ nk.**

MATERIALS

- Worktext pp. 17–19
- Routine Cards 1, 2, 7
- Letter tiles

Set the scene Remind students that in many words consonants work together to spell one or more sounds. Today we will learn to read and spell words that end with the letters **ck, dge, ng,** and **nk.**

Routine **1. Connect Sound to Spelling** Help students connect today's lesson to previously learned sound-spellings. Write *cap* and *kit.* What do you know about the beginning letter sounds in these words? Remind students that they have learned to read words with /k/ spelled *c* and /k/ spelled *k.* In this lesson, you'll learn to connect /k/ with *ck* and to blend words that end in *ck.*

2. Model and Give Examples Write *ck* and point to the letters. What is the sound for these letters? Have students say /k/ several times with you. Write and say *quick.* Tell students that, when words end with the sound /k/, the sound is often spelled by the letters *ck.*

3. Model Blending Write *track* beneath *quick.* Point to both words. Now let's read these words that end with *ck.* Run your hand under each letter as you blend each word sound-by-sound: /kw//i//k/, *quick;* /t//r//a//k/, *track.* Have students blend each word with you and without you. Then invite students to think about the meanings of these words. Ask them to use each word in a sentence to make its meaning clear. Encourage students to identify different possible meanings of *track* (for example, *a railroad track, a deer track in the snow, a race around a track, to track the cost of gas*).

Mini-Lesson 1 Final /k/ *ck*

Remind students that...

- Many words end with final **/k/** spelled *ck.*

Word List

attack	deck
brick	stick
crack	flock

Guide Practice

Repeat the routine above to help students read and spell words that end with **/k/ ck.** Write *block* and circle the letters *ck.* What sound do these letters stand for? Say /k/ with students. Run your hand under *bl* as you say the blend: /b//l/. Add *o*, say its sound, and blend the first two sounds: /b//l//o/. Then point to *ck* and blend the whole word: /b//l//o//k/. Have students blend with you. Repeat the process to introduce the remaining words. Encourage students to discuss the meaning(s) of each word.

block	check	struck	wreck

If... students cannot read a word,

then... remind them that *ck* often spells the sound /k/. Say the first sound and write its spelling. Continue until the entire word has been written (Routine Card 7).

On Their Own For more practice, use Worktext p. 17. In addition, help students use letter tiles to spell and read the words on the Word List. Use each word in a sentence to help students understand its meaning.

Mini-Lesson 2 Final /j/ *dge*

Remind students that...
- Consonants can work together to spell one final sound.
- The sound /j/ spelled *dge* is used at the end of many words.

Word List

bridge	budge
dodge	pledge
fudge	smudge

Guide Practice

Use sound-by-sound blending strategies (Routine Cards 1, 2) to help students connect /j/ with *dge* and to blend words that end with *dge*. Write the first two words below and say them aloud several times. What sound do you hear at the end of each word? What letters spell that sound? Point to *dge* as students repeat the sound /j/. Run your hand under the words as you and students say them:

/b//a//j/, *badge;* /g//r//u//j/, *grudge.* Repeat the process with the remaining pair of words. Discuss each word's meaning with students. Help them make up a sentence that uses each word.

badge	grudge	knowledge	lodge

If... students cannot read a word,

then... write each letter, blend, or digraph and ask for its sound(s). Have students blend the word with and without you.

On Their Own See Worktext p. 18 and the Word List for additional practice with words with *dge.* Help students build each word with letter tiles. Work together to use each word in a sentence.

Mini-Lesson 3 Final /ng/ *ng* and /ngk/ *nk*

Remind students that...
- Final sounds can be spelled with a combination of letters.
- The sounds /ng/ spelled *ng* and /ngk/ spelled *nk* are used at the end of many words.
- Digraphs are two consecutive letters that stand for a single sound, such as *sh* or *th*.

Word List

among	chipmunk
cling	sink
swing	yank

Guide Practice

Remind students that they have learned to read words that end with two consonant sounds blended together, such as *jump* and *most.* Today we will learn about words that end with the letters *ng* and *nk.* Write *bring, hang,* and *wrong.* What do you notice about how all of these words

end? Have students say /ng/ several times as you point to *ng.* Run your hand under the letters as you blend each whole word: /b//r//i//ng/, *bring;* /h//a//ng/, *hang;* /r//o//ng/, *wrong.* Repeat the procedure to introduce /ngk/ spelled *nk* in the remaining words. Monitor students' understanding of the words' meanings.

bring	hang	wrong
blank	shrink	trunk

If... students have difficulty reading a word,

then... remind them to think about the sound(s) for each spelling they see. Have them blend the word in their heads before they read it aloud.

On Their Own For additional practice, use Worktext p. 19 and the Word List. Discuss each word's meaning and help students use each word in a sentence.

Short Vowel Phonograms

Objectives:
- Teach concept of phonograms.
- Introduce short *a* phonograms.
- Introduce short *o* and *i* phonograms.
- Introduce short *u* and *e* phonograms.

MATERIALS
- Worktext pp. 20–22
- Routine Cards 1, 2, 4
- Letter tiles

Set the scene Write *cat.* Ask students to brainstorm words that rhyme with *cat.* (Possible answers might include *bat, flat,* or *sat.*) These words are part of the same word family. A word family is a group of words that rhyme and share the same vowel and the letters that follow it. We call them *phonograms.* Point to the letters *at. Cat* and words that rhyme with *cat* have the short *a* sound, **/a/,** spelled with **a.** Today you will learn to spell and read words in several common word families that begin with short vowels.

Routine **1. Connect** Write *back* and *flap.* Read them aloud. Tell students that they will learn a new way to read these words and other words in the same word family by identifying the word parts *-ack* and *-ap.* Knowing how to read *-ack* and *-ap* can help you read many words with these word parts.

2. Model and Give Examples Point to *back.* This word has two parts. Cover the word part *-ack* and point to *b.* Say its sound: /b/. Then cover *b* and say *-ack* aloud. Repeat the procedure with *flap* and the word part *-ap.*

3. Model Blending Run your hand under *back* again. *Back* is one of many words with the word part *-ack.* When you see a word that ends with *-ack,* notice the word part that comes before the vowel and then say the two word parts one after the other. In this word, the parts are /b/ and *-ack.* Read it with me: /b/, *-ack, back.* Erase *b* and write *s.* How do you say this word? Blend *sack* with children. Repeat with *snack* and *quack.* Follow the same procedure to read *flap* and the word part *-ap* and the words *clap, sap,* and *snap.* Encourage students to name other words that end with *-ack* and *-ap.* Discuss their meanings.

Mini-Lesson 1 Short *a* Phonograms

Remind students that...
- A phonogram is part of a word made up of a vowel and all the letters that follow it, as *-ack* in *back, black, stack.*
- Many words include short *a* phonograms, such as *-ab, -ack, -ad, -ag, -am, -ap, -at,* and *-ank.*

Word List
scab, crab, grab	swam, clam, wham
rack, crack, black	chap, clap, zap
glad, mad, had	flat, hat, bat
brag, flag, snag	prank, sank, plank

Guide Practice
Explain that today students will learn to read words with *-ab, -ack, -ad,* and *-ag.* Write *grab. Grab* is one of many words with the word part *-ab.* When you see a word with *-ab* at the end, look at the word part that comes before the vowel and say the word parts one after the other.

Have students identify the two parts: /g/ /r/ and *-ab.* Have them read the word with you: /g/ /r/, *-ab, grab.* Erase *gr* and write *cr* to form the word *crab,* and blend the word with students. Follow the same procedure to introduce the short *a* phonograms in the other words below. Discuss the meaning of each word together as a class.

grab, crab	rack, snack
pad, sad	bag, drag

Repeat the procedure with the short *a* phonograms *-am, -ap, -at,* and *-ank* in the words below.

jam, slam	snap, wrap
bat, chat	sank, crank

If... students cannot read a word,

then... have them identify one part at a time as you cover the remaining part (Routine Card 4).

On Their Own For additional practice, use Worktext p. 20 and the Word List. Help students use each word in a sentence.

Mini-Lesson 2 — Short *o* and *i* Phonograms

Remind students that…

- A phonogram is part of a word made up of a vowel and all the letters that follow it, as *-ack* in *back, black, stack.*
- Many words include short *o* phonograms, such as *-ob, -ock, -op,* and *-ot.*
- Many words include short *i* phonograms, such as *-ick, -ill, -in, -ing,* and *-ip.*

Word List

rob, slob	bill, thrill
sock, clock	bin, twin
pop, flop	wing, bring
spot, trot	tip, snip
trick, chick	

Guide Practice

Use the routine on the previous page to introduce common short *o* and short *i* phonograms. Write the words below with the word parts *-ob, -ock, -op,* and *-ot.* When you see a word with one of these word parts, look at the word part that comes before *-ob, -ock, -op,* and *-ot.* Read the two word parts, one after the other. Model segmenting each word. Have students read each word with you and use it in a sentence to clarify its meaning. As a group, try to think of at least two other words that rhyme with each word.

glob, job	flock, block	crop, stop	plot, cot

Repeat the process to introduce these short *i* phonograms: *-ick, -ill, -in, -ing,* and *-ip.*

sick, flick	will, chill	spin, thin
swing, king	trip, slip	

If… students cannot read a word,

then… model blending the parts one after the other without pausing (Routine Cards 1, 2, 4).

On Their Own Use Worktext p. 21 and the Word List for additional practice. Challenge students to use each word in a sentence.

Mini-Lesson 3 — Short *u* and *e* Phonograms

Remind students that…

- A phonogram is part of a word made up of a vowel and all the letters that follow it, as *-ack* in *back, black, stack.*
- Many words include short *u* phonograms, such as *-ug, -um, -unk,* and *-ut.*
- Many words include short *e* phonograms, such as *-eck, -ed, -ell,* and *-est.*

Word List

plug, drug	speck, deck
drum, plum	sled, red
trunk, stunk	cell, smell
hut, cut	quest, pest

Guide Practice

Remind students that they have learned many words with short *u* and short *e* sounds, such as *bus* and *jet.* Repeat step 3 of the routine on the previous page to introduce the phonogram *-ug,* using the words *plug* and *snug.* Follow the same procedure to introduce the other words below with *-ug, -um, -unk,* and *-ut.* Develop word meaning by asking questions and using words in sentences.

plug, snug	swum, glum
chunk, skunk	strut, shut

Repeat the process with the words below to introduce the phonograms *-eck, -ed, -ell,* and *-est.*

fleck, wreck	sped, fed
swell, bell	pest, nest

If… students have difficulty reading a word,

then… help them read the word parts as you run your hand beneath them (Routine Card 4).

On Their Own Have students complete Worktext p. 22. Also, have students use letter tiles to build and read the Word List words. Take turns using each word in a sentence.

Phonics and Decoding Lesson 8
More Consonant Sounds

Objectives:
- Teach concept of soft consonant sounds.
- Introduce soft **c** sound **/s/**.
- Introduce soft **g** sound **/j/**.
- Introduce **/z/ s** sound.

MATERIALS
- Worktext pp. 23–25
- Routine Cards 1, 2
- Letter tiles

Set the scene Remind students that they have learned to read words that contain the sound **/s/** spelled *s* (*song*), the sound **/j/** spelled *j* (*jug*), and the sound **/z/** spelled *z* (*zoo*). Today we will learn new spellings for these sounds.

Routine **1. Connect Sound to Spelling** Help students connect today's lesson to previously learned sound-spellings. Write *sun, boys,* and *seem.* Read the words aloud, slowly blending each sound. What letter do these words have in common? Yes, the sound /s/ spelled *s* is in all three words. In today's lesson, you'll learn to spell and read words with /s/ spelled *c*.

2. Model and Give Examples Write *cent.* This word is another word for penny. Ask a volunteer to say it aloud. Yes, this is *cent.* Point to *ce.* When *c* is followed by *e, c* usually stands for /s/. Have students say /s/ with you as you run your hand under *ce.* Repeat the procedure to explain that *c* followed by *i* can also stand for /s/, as in *city.*

3. Model Blending Point to *cent* and *city.* Run your hand under each word as you blend the sounds to say the word: /s//e//nt/, *cent;* /s//i//t//ē/, *city.* Ask students which letters spell the /s/ sound in these words. Remember, when you see the letter *c* followed by *e* or *i,* try the sound /s/ for the *c.* The *c* sound in *cent* and *city* is called a soft *c* sound. Have volunteers use each word in a sentence that demonstrates its meaning. Finally, challenge students to look around the room and think of another word which contains /s/ spelled *c* followed by *e* or *i* (for example, *center, ceiling,* or *circle*).

Mini-Lesson 1 — Soft *c* Consonant Sound /s/

Remind students that...
- Some sounds can be spelled in more than one way.
- *C* followed by *e* or *i* usually stands for /s/.

Word List

celery	once
cereal	cinch
circle	citizen

Guide Practice

Help students understand that the sound **/s/** can be spelled **c** by using the routine above. Write *cement* and *center.* Say the words aloud several times. What sound do you hear at the beginning of these words? When *c* is followed by *e* or *i,* it stands for the sound /s/. Have students blend each word as you point to each spelling and say its sound. Use each word in a sentence and discuss its meaning. Then repeat the procedure to model the remaining words below.

cement	center	excite	cider
circus	pencil		

If... students cannot read a word,
then... model blending for decodable words (Routine Cards 1, 2).

On Their Own Have students complete Worktext p. 23. In addition, provide students with letter tiles to spell and read the words on the Word List. Help students use each word in a sentence.

Mini-Lesson 2 — Soft *g* Consonant Sound /j/

Remind students that...
• Some sounds can be spelled in more than one way.
• Many words contain the soft **g** sound **/j/** (spelled *j* or *g*).

Word List

germ	logic
gem	region
gentle	tragic

Guide Practice
Use the routine on the previous page to connect **/j/** with **g.** You know many words that begin with the sound /j/ spelled with *j*. Write and say *jet* and point to *j*. Invite volunteers to identify other words or names with the sound /j/ spelled *j* (for example, *jot, June, Julie*). Today you'll learn to spell and read words with /j/ spelled *g* followed by *e* or *i*. Write *gem*. Say it aloud. Did you hear the final /j/? When *g* is followed by *e* or *i*, it often spells

the sound /j/. Blend the word with me: /g//e//m/. Repeat this procedure to model the remaining words below. Encourage discussion of the meaning of each word.

genius	gentle	village	engine
giant	giraffe		

If... students cannot read a word,
then... point to *g* followed by *e* or *i* as you say the sound /j/ with students several times.

On Their Own Use Worktext p. 24 and the Word List for additional practice with words with a soft *g* sound. Work together to use each word in a sentence.

Mini-Lesson 3 — Consonant Sound *s* /z/

Remind students that...
• Some sounds can be spelled in more than one way.
• Many words contain the sound **/z/ s.**

Word List

flags	pills
frogs	those
has	yells

Guide Practice
Introduce students to the sound **/z/** spelled **s.** Remember that some consonant sounds can be spelled in different ways. Write *zebra* and *his*. Say each word. Ask students to identify the first sound in *zebra* and the last sound in *his*. The sound /z/ can be spelled with *z* (point to *zebra*). It can also be spelled with *s* (point to *his*). One at a time, write each remaining word below. Repeat step 3 of the

routine to model blending its sounds. Have students blend each word. Discuss word meanings. Invite students to work in pairs to use two of the words in a sentence.

his	hides	rise	tease	use

If... students cannot read a word,
then... suggest they think about the sound(s) for each spelling they see. Have them blend the word in their heads before they read it aloud.

On Their Own For additional practice, use Worktext p. 25 and the Word List. Use each word in a sentence to help students understand its meaning.

Phonics and Decoding Lesson 9
Long Vowels

Objectives:
- Teach concept of long vowel sounds.
- Introduce long *a* spelled *a_e*.
- Introduce long *i* spelled *i_e*.
- Introduce long *o* spelled *o_e*.

MATERIALS
- Worktext pp. 26–28
- Routine Cards 1, 2, 7
- Letter tiles

Set the scene Remind students that words are made up of both consonant and vowel sounds. You learned how to read words with short vowel sounds. In this lesson, you will learn to read words with long vowel sounds /ā/, /ī/, and /ō/.

Routine **1. Connect Sound to Spelling** Remind students that they have studied words with short *a*. Write *at* and *slam*. Ask students to read these words. Listen for the short *a* sound in these words. Remember, it sounds like /a/. The long *a* sound is /ā/. Today you will learn to blend words with the long *a* sound.

2. Model and Give Examples Write and say *late*. What vowel sound do you hear? The word *late* has a long *a* sound. Point to *a* in *late* and have students repeat /ā/ several times. Beneath *late*, write *a_e*. The long *a* sound, /ā/, can be spelled *a_e*. The letter *e* gives the vowel *a* its long sound, and the blank (point to it) shows where a consonant goes.

3. Model Blending Point to *a_e* again and have students say /ā/. Then write *f* before *a* and blend the sounds: /f//ā/. Write *m* in the blank. Listen as I blend this word: /f//ā//m/, *fame*. Have students blend the word. Ask a volunteer to use *fame* in a sentence. Then challenge students to brainstorm words that rhyme with *fame* and share the same *a_e* spelling pattern (such as *blame, came*). Discuss the meanings of those words.

Mini-Lesson 1 — Long *a* (spelled *a_e*)

Remind students that...
- A long vowel sound is one that is the same as the name of a vowel letter—*a, e, i, o,* and *u.*
- Many words contain the long *a* sound, /ā/, spelled *a_e.*

Word List
blame	quake
date	shade
plate	trace

Guide Practice
Help students read words with /ā/ spelled *a_e* by using the routine above. Write *a_e*. Point to *a_e* and have students say the sound with you: /ā/. Write *ch* before *a*. Blend these sounds with me: /ch//ā/. Then write *s* in the blank and say its sound. Let's blend the word together: /ch//ā//s/. Remember, when you see the spelling pattern *a_e* in a word, try the long *a* sound, /ā/. Follow this procedure to model the remaining words below. Begin each word by writing the vowel spelling *a_e* as a unit. Encourage students to discuss the meanings and use each word in a sentence.

chase   flake   gaze   page   wade

If... students cannot read a word,
then... say each sound as you write its spelling. Model blending the sounds without pausing (Routine Cards 1, 7).

On Their Own For more practice, use Worktext p. 26. Provide additional practice with the Word List. Help students use letter tiles to spell and read each word.

Mini-Lesson 2 — Long *i* (spelled *i_e*)

Remind students that...
- A long vowel sound is a vowel sound that is the same as the name of a vowel letter—*a, e, i, o,* and *u.*
- Many words contain the long *i* sound, /ī/, spelled *i_e.*

Word List
file	prize
glide	kite
lime	whine

Guide Practice
Write *i_e* and have students say its sound: /ī/. Today we will blend words with this long *i* spelling pattern. Write *ch* and say its sound: /ch/. Write *m* in the blank and say its sound. Then blend the whole word *chime,* pointing to *i* and *e* as you say /ī/. Blend this word with me: /ch//ī//m/. Follow this procedure to model blending the remaining

words below. Encourage discussion of the meaning of each word. Ask pairs of students to brainstorm more words with the *i_e* spelling pattern.

chime   strike   twine   while   wipe

If... students have difficulty reading a word,
then... point to the *i* and remind students that when they see the spelling *i_ e* in a word, they should try the sound /ī/. Help students use sound-by-sound blending strategies to say the word (Routine Cards 1, 2).

On Their Own See Worktext p. 27 and the Word List for additional practice. Help students think of a sentence that uses each word on the Word List.

Mini-Lesson 3 — Long *o* (spelled *o_e*)

Remind students that...
- A long vowel sound is a vowel sound that is the same as the name of a vowel letter—*a, e, i, o,* and *u.*
- Many words contain the long *o* sound, /ō/, spelled *o_e.*

Word List
close	quote
froze	smoke
pole	zone

Guide Practice
To help students connect /ō/ with *o_e* and blend words with the long *o* spelling pattern, write and say *not.* What do you know about the vowel sound in *not?* (The sound is short *o.*) Add *e. Note* has a long *o* sound. Write *o_e* and say its sound: /ō/. The letter *e* gives the vowel *o* its long sound. The blank shows where a consonant will go. Write *o_e* and say its sound: /ō/. Write *br* and have

students blend the sounds: /b//r//o/. Write *k* in the blank and say its sound. Then blend the whole word with students: /b//r//ō//k/, *broke.* Follow this procedure to model the remaining words below. Discuss the meaning of each word.

broke   cone   drove   rope   throne

If... students have difficulty reading a word,
then... model blending the sounds in the word slowly as you run your hand under each sound-spelling.

On Their Own For more practice, use the Word List and Worktext p. 28. Help students use each word in a sentence to clarify its meaning.

Phonics and Decoding Lesson 10
Other Long Vowel Patterns

Objectives:
- Teach concept of long vowel sounds.
- Introduce long *u* spelled *u_e* and long *e* spelled *e_e*.
- Introduce long *e, o, i* spelled *e, o, i*.
- Introduce long *i* and long *e* spelled *y*.
- Introduce long *a* spelled *eigh*.

MATERIALS
- Worktext pp. 29–31
- Routine Cards 1, 2, 7, 8
- Letter tiles

Set the scene Remind students that they have learned how to read many words with short and long vowel sounds. Give example words, such as *fat* (short *a*) and *fate* (long *a*). Today we will learn to read and spell words with long *u* spelled *u_e,* long *e* spelled *e_e,* and long *a* spelled *eigh.*

Routine **1. Connect Sound to Spelling** Connect today's lesson to previously learned sound-spellings. Write *wave, dine,* and *stole.* Circle the vowel in each word and say each word aloud several times. The vowels in these words are long. Say /ā/, /ī/, and /ō/. Notice that each word ends in a vowel, consonant, vowel pattern. Underline the last three letters of each word. In this lesson you will learn to spell and read words with /ū/ spelled *u_e* and /ē/ spelled *e_e.*

2. Model and Give Examples Write *u_e.* Have students say /ū/ as you point to the letters. The letter *e* gives the vowel *u* its long sound. Be sure students understand that the blank shows where a consonant will go. Repeat the procedure to introduce /ē/ spelled *e_e.* Many words include these spelling patterns.

3. Model Blending Point to *u_e* and say its sound again: /ū/. Write *c* and blend the sounds: /k//ū/. Write *t* in the blank and say /t/. Run your hand under the whole word as you blend it: /k//ū//t/, *cute.* Have students blend the word with you. Follow this procedure to model the long *e* sound spelled *e_e,* as in *theme.* Invite volunteers to discuss the meaning of each word. Say a sentence using each word.

Mini-Lesson 1 — Long *u* (spelled *u_e*) and Long *e* (spelled *e_e*)

Remind students that...
- Vowel sounds can be short or long.
- Many words contain the long *u* sound, spelled *u_e,* and the long *e* sound, spelled *e_e.*

Word List

cute	complete
mule	eve
use	these

Guide Practice
Repeat the routine above to introduce words that end with *u_e* and *e_e.* Write and read aloud this sentence: *The ice cube fell.* Run your hand beneath the *ube* in *cube.* When you see the spelling *u_e* in a word, try the long *u* sound, /ū/. Write *u_e* and say /u/. The letter *e* gives the vowel *u* its long sound. The blank shows where a consonant goes. Blend the sounds in *cube* with

students: /k//ū//b/, *cube.* Follow this procedure to model *fume* and *huge.* Then write *e_e* and introduce the long *e* sound in the remaining words. Discuss the meaning(s) of each word.

cube	fume	huge	scheme
scene	these		

If... students cannot read a word,
then... say each sound and write its spelling. Model blending the sounds (Routine Cards 1, 7).

On Their Own For more practice, have students complete Worktext p. 29. Have students use letter tiles to spell and read the words on the Word List. Help students use each word in a sentence.

Mini-Lesson 2 — Long *e* (spelled *e*), Long *o* (spelled *o*), and Long *i* (spelled *i*)

Remind students that...
- Vowel sounds can be short or long.
- Many words use *e* to spell /ē/, *o* to spell /ō/, or *i* to spell /ī/.

Word List

he	yo-yo
we	blind
post	child

Guide Practice
Use this lesson to help students connect /ē/ with *e*, /ō/ with *o*, and /ī/ with *i*. Connect this lesson to previously learned sound-spellings by writing *these*, *vote*, and *bite*. Say the words aloud. Point to the first vowel in each word. What do you know about the vowel sounds in these words? (The vowels are long; they say their names.)

Remind students that these long vowel sounds can be spelled in different ways. Write *e* and say /ē/. Then write *sh*. Blend the whole word: /sh//ē/. Follow this procedure to model the long *o* and long *i* sounds in the remaining words. Discuss the meaning(s) of any unfamiliar words.

she   bolt   hi   host   grind

If... students have difficulty reading a word,
then... model whole-word blending (Routine Card 2).

On Their Own See Worktext p. 30 and the Word List for additional practice. Have students work together to use each word in a sentence.

Mini-Lesson 3 — Long *i* and Long *e* (spelled *y*) and Long *a* (spelled *eigh*)

Remind students that...
- Vowel sounds can be short or long.
- Many words end with the sounds /ī/ and /ē/ spelled *y*.
- In some words, the sound /ā/ is spelled *eigh*.

Word List

pry	neighbor
sky	sleigh
bunny	weight
lady	

Guide Practice
Explain that today students will learn different ways to spell long *i*, long *e*, and long *a* sounds. Write *spy* and *why*. Point to *y* and have students repeat /ī/. Model blending the words. When the letter *y* comes at the end of a one-syllable word, *y* usually spells /ī/. Write *sly* and *hobby*. How many syllables are in these words? When *y*

comes at the end of a word with more than one syllable, it usually spells /ē/. Point to *y* and say /ē/. Blend the words together. Then write and say *eight* and *weigh*. Point to *eigh* and say /ā/. In these words, the long *a* sound is spelled *eigh*. Model blending these words with students. Have students use each word in a sentence.

spy   why   hobby
eight   weigh

If... students have difficulty reading a word,
then... touch under the letter(s) while you say the sound.

On Their Own For additional practice, use Worktext p. 31 and the Word List. Discuss the meaning of each word.

Phonics and Decoding Lesson 11
Endings

Objectives:
- Teach concept of inflected endings.
- Introduce endings *-s, -es.*
- Introduce ending *-ed.*
- Introduce ending *-ing.*

MATERIALS
- Worktext pp. 32–34
- Routine Cards 1, 2, 4, 7
- Letter tiles

Set the scene Tell students that in this lesson they will learn to add endings to words they know to make new words. Today we will learn to read words with the endings *-s, -es, -ed,* and *-ing.* When we add *-s* or *-es* to some words, we make the words plural, or more than one. When we add *-ed* or *-ing* to verbs such as *jump* and *talk* we change when those actions happen. For example, the ending *-ed* shows that the action happened in the past.

Routine

1. Connect Write *plant* and *hog.* Ask volunteers to say each word aloud and explain its meaning. You know how to read these words. In this lesson, we will learn to make and read new words by adding the letter *s* to these and other words.

2. Model and Give Examples Point to *plant* and have students say it with you. We can add the word part *-s* to make a new word. Add *-s* to form *plants.* Cover the word part *-s.* Read the base word *plant.* Then cover *plant* and point to the word part *-s.* Ask students what sound *s* stands for. Say /s/. Then say the new word: *plants.*

3. Model Blending Point to the word part *-s.* When you see a word with *-s* at the end, notice the two parts. In *plants,* the parts are *plant* and *-s.* Read them one after the other: *plant, s, plants.* Next, add *-s* to *hog.* Ask students to identify the word's two parts (*hog, -s*). The *-s* in *hogs* spells the sound /z/. Have students say the word with you: *hog, s, hogs.* Ask volunteers to use each word in a sentence. When we add the word part *-s* to the end of a word, sometimes it stands for the sound /s/, as in *plants* or *locks.* Sometimes it stands for the sound /z/, as in *hogs* or *yells.*

Mini-Lesson 1 Endings *-s, -es*

Remind students that...
- Many words are made up of smaller word parts.
- Many words end with the word parts *-s* and *-es.*

Word List

socks	buses
books	lunches
clocks	foxes

Guide Practice

Tell students that today they will learn to make new words by adding *-s* and *-es* to words they know. Write *block.* Blend it with students. Add *-s.* This word has two parts. Point to the parts as you and students say them: *block, s, blocks.* Then discuss its meanings (for example, *a baby's blocks, a city block*). Repeat the procedure with the other words below. In which word does the letter *s* stand for the /z/, not the /s/, sound? (*songs*)

blocks	songs	cars	hats

If a word ends with the letters *s* or *x*, you can make a new word by adding the word part *-es.* Follow the procedure above to help students read the words below.

bosses	dresses	boxes	foxes

If... students cannot read a word,
then... have them identify one part at a time as you cover the remaining part.

On Their Own Have students complete Worktext p. 32. Provide additional practice with *-s* and *-es* endings with the Word List words.

 **Ending -ed**

Remind students that...
- Many words are made up of smaller word parts.
- Many words end with the word part *-ed.*

Word List

blushed	pumped
waited	rolled
guessed	tricked

Guide Practice

Use the routine to help students make and read words with the word part *-ed.* Write *blasted* and *clicked.* What two word parts do these words have? If students have difficulty identifying parts, point to *blast* and *click* as you cover *-ed.* Then cover *blast* and *click* as you point to *-ed.* Say the parts one after the other: *blast, ed, blasted; click, ed, clicked.* Have students say the words. What do you notice about the sound of the word part *-ed* in

each word? (In *blasted* it spells /d/. In *clicked* it spells /t/.) Point out that adding *-ed* sometimes adds a syllable to a word, such as in *blasted.* Follow this procedure to read the remaining words. Discuss the words' meanings as needed.

blasted   clicked   walked   scowled

If... students have difficulty reading a word,

then... help them blend the sounds of the base word before they read the word part *-ed* (Routine Cards 1, 2).

On Their Own See Worktext p. 33 and the Word List for more practice. Help students use letter tiles to spell the words. Use each word in a sentence.

Mini-Lesson 3 Ending -ing

Remind students that...
- Many words are made up of smaller word parts.
- Many words end with the word part *-ing.*

Word List

finding	sprinting
farming	trusting
snacking	yanking

Guide Practice

Explain that in this lesson students will learn about adding the word part *-ing* to words. Write *flashing.* Ask students to identify the base word (*flash*). Blend it with students. Point to the word part *-ing* and say it aloud. Notice the two parts in this word. To say the word, read the parts one after the other. Point to *flashing.* Read with me: *flash, ing, flashing.* Follow this procedure to help students

read the remaining words. Ask a volunteer to use each word in a sentence. Invite discussion of the meaning of each word.

flashing   looking   limping
pressing   stomping

If... students have difficulty reading a word,

then... model identifying word parts. Then read the word as you run your hand beneath the parts (Routine Card 4).

On Their Own For more practice, use the Word List and Worktext p. 34. To provide practice with spelling, have students use letter tiles to spell the words (Routine Card 7). Work together to use each word in a sentence.

Phonics and Decoding Lesson 12
Syllable Patterns

Objectives:
- Teach concept of syllable patterns.
- Introduce syllable pattern **VC/CV.**
- Introduce syllable pattern **V/CV.**
- Introduce syllable pattern **VC/V.**

MATERIALS
- Worktext pp. 35–37
- Routine Cards 1, 4
- Letter tiles

Set the scene Remind students that a syllable is a word part that contains a single vowel sound. Explain that in this lesson they will learn to read words with three common syllable patterns: **VC/CV, V/CV,** and **VC/V.**

Routine **1. Connect** Help students connect today's lesson to previous learning. Write and say *eating* several times, slowly to distinguish each syllable. What are the syllables in this word? (*eat, ing*) The first syllable ends at the end of the base word, *eat.* Today you will learn to divide two-syllable words that have two consonants in the middle.

2. Model and Give Examples Write and say *magnet* several times. *Magnet* has two syllables. Ask students to identify the two consonants in the middle of *magnet.* (*g, n*) *Magnet* follows the vowel-consonant-consonant-vowel spelling pattern. Point to *a, g, n,* and *e.* To break the word into two smaller parts, divide *magnet* between the two consonants. Cover *net* and say *mag* aloud. Then cover *mag* and read *net* aloud.

3. Model Blending Write *admire.* When you see a word with two consonants in the middle, divide the word into syllables between the two consonants. Draw a line between *d* and *m.* Read the syllables one after the other with students: *ad, mire, admire.* Repeat the process with *happen.* Say *admire, magnet,* and *happen.* What do you notice about the sound of the vowel *a* in the first syllable of these words? (It has the short *a* sound /a/.) In words with the VC/CV pattern, the first syllable often has a short vowel sound. Encourage students to use each word in a sentence.

Mini-Lesson 1 — Syllable Pattern VC/CV

Remind students that...
- Some words can be broken into smaller word parts.
- A syllable is a word part that contains a single vowel sound.
- Many words contain the syllable pattern **VC/CV.**

Word List
convince	mitten
fifteen	trumpet
frantic	welcome

Guide Practice
This lesson helps students read words with the **VC/CV** syllable pattern. Write *escape* and *hidden* and say the words several times. How many syllables does each word have? What two consonants are in the middle of each word? Point to *sc* in *escape* and *dd* in *hidden.* What do you notice about the two consonants in these words?

(In *escape* the two consonants are different letters. In *hidden,* they are the same.)

In words with two consonants in the middle, remember to divide the word after the first consonant. Read the syllables one after the other to say the word: *es, cape, escape; hid, den, hidden.* Repeat the process with the remaining word below. Discuss their meanings.

escape   hidden   until

If... students cannot read a word,
then... identify its two syllables and model reading one after the other (Routine Card 4).

On Their Own Have students complete Worktext p. 35. In addition, use the Word List for more practice with VC/CV words. Help students use letter tiles to build words.

Mini-Lesson 2 — Syllable Pattern V/CV

Remind students that...
- Some words can be broken into smaller word parts.
- A syllable is a word part that contains a single vowel sound.
- Many words contain the syllable pattern **V/CV**.

Word List
bonus	moment
famous	tulip
local	final

Guide Practice
Introduce students to words that contain the syllable pattern **V/CV**. Write and say *basic.* This word has two syllables. Point to *s.* Words with the V/CV pattern have only one consonant between vowels. In a word with a consonant between two vowels, the consonant usually goes with the second syllable. Draw a line between *a* and *s.* Read the syllables: *ba, sic, basic.* What do you notice about the sound of *a* in the first syllable? (It is /ā/.)

In a two-syllable word with the V/CV pattern, the first syllable usually has a long vowel sound. Repeat the process with the remaining words. Have students discuss their meanings.

basic   donate   flavor   private

If... students cannot read a word,

then... exaggerate the long vowel sound in the first syllable as you model blending the syllables (Routine Cards 1, 4).

On Their Own Use Worktext p. 36 and the Word List for additional practice. Have students work together to use each word in a sentence.

Mini-Lesson 3 — Syllable Pattern VC/V

Remind students that...
- Some words can be broken into smaller word parts.
- A syllable is a word part that contains a single vowel sound.
- Many words contain the syllable pattern **VC/V**.

Word List
clever	novel
exit	spinach
lizard	timid

Guide Practice
Focus students on words with the syllable pattern **VC/V**. Remind students that they learned how to read words with the syllable pattern V/CV. Write and say *pupil.* The consonant (point to the second *p*) goes with the second syllable, making the first vowel long, /ū/. Say *pupil.*

Then write *cabin.* Guide students through the same procedure to read *cabin.* If I divide *cabin* before the *b,* the *a* will have a long sound, /ā/. Say /k//ā//b//ə//n/. That doesn't sound right. Let's try dividing the word after the *b.* That makes the *a* sound short: /k//a//b//ə//n/. That sounds right: *cab, in, cabin.* Repeat the procedure to read and identify the syllables in the remaining words. Discuss each word's meaning.

cabin   finish   dragon   habit   honor

If... students cannot read a word,

then... have them blend one syllable as you cover the other one (Routine Card 4).

On Their Own Give students more practice with the Word List and Worktext p. 37. Monitor students' understanding of the meaning of the words.

Phonics and Decoding Lesson 13
R-Controlled Vowels

Objectives:
- Teach concept of r-controlled vowels.
- Introduce /är/ *ar*.
- Introduce /ôr/ *or, ore, oar.*
- Introduce /èr/ *er, ir, ur.*

MATERIALS
- Worktext pp. 38–40
- Routine Cards 1, 2, 5
- Letter tiles

Set the scene Explain that in this lesson students will practice reading words in which a vowel is followed by the letter *r.* You have learned that vowels can stand for different sounds. When a vowel is followed by *r,* it stands for a special sound.

Routine **1. Connect Sound to Spelling** Connect today's lesson to students' knowledge of vowel sounds. Write and say *chat* and *had* several times. What do you notice about the sound *a* stands for in these words? (It stands for the short *a* sound, /a/.) Today we will learn about the special sound the vowel *a* makes when it is followed by the letter *r.* It is neither long nor short.

2. Model and Give Examples Beneath *chat* and *had,* write *chart* and *hard.* Listen to how the sound of the letter *a* changes when we add the letter *r* after *a.* Point to each pair of words and have students say them with you: *chat, chart; had, hard.* The letters *ar* (point to them) in these words spell the sound /är/. Have students say /är/ several times as you point to *ar.*

3. Model Blending Have students blend the words with you. Point to each spelling as you say its sound: /ch//är//t/, /h//är//d/. When you see the spelling *ar* in a word, what sound should you try? (/är/) Encourage pairs of students to brainstorm words that contain the sound /är/ spelled *ar* and rhyme with *chart* and *hard* (for example, *part, smart, start, dart, yard, regard, card, guard*). Have them explain what each word means and use it in a sentence.

Mini-Lesson 1 — *R*-Controlled Vowel /är/ *ar*

Remind students that...
- Consonants and vowels may join together to spell a new sound.
- An *r*-controlled vowel sound is the sound of a vowel immediately followed by *r* in the same syllable.
- Many words contain the sound /är/ spelled *ar.*

Word List

arch	mark
guitar	shark
harm	snarl

Guide Practice
Use the routine to help students connect /är/ with *ar.* Write *bark.* Point to the letters *ar.* What sound do the letters *ar* stand for? Have students say /är/ with you several times. When you see the spelling *ar* in a word, try the sound /är/. Then have students blend the whole word with you: /b//är//k/. Develop word meaning by asking questions. What does *bark* mean in this sentence: *The tree's bark feels rough.* What other meanings of *bark* do you know? (for example, *a dog's bark*) Repeat the procedure to guide practice with the remaining words below.

bark	charm	marble	remark	scarf

If... students cannot read words with the letters *ar,*
then... remind them that *ar* stands for the sound /är/. Run your finger along each sound-spelling as you model blending the whole word (Routine Card 2).

On Their Own For additional practice, use Worktext p. 38. Have students use letter tiles to build and read words on the Word List. Discuss word meanings.

Mini-Lesson 2 R-Controlled Vowel /ôr/ *or, ore, oar*

Remind students that...

- Consonants and vowels may join together to spell a new sound.
- An *r*-controlled vowel sound is the sound of a vowel immediately followed by *r* in the same syllable.
- Many words contain the sound /ôr/ spelled *or, ore, oar*.

Word List

airport	bore	boar
fort	swore	coarse

Guide Practice

Remind students that when the letter *r* follows a vowel, the vowel usually changes its sound. Write *fan* and *far* and have students compare the sounds of *a* in each. Today you'll read words with /ôr/.

The sound /ôr/ can be spelled with several different letter combinations. Write *or, ore,* and *oar.* Say /ôr/ as you point to each group of letters. Beneath those, write *for, chore,* and *soar.* Circle the *or, ore,* and *oar* spellings as students repeat the sound /ôr/. Run your hand under the words as you blend them. Ask volunteers to use each word in a sentence. Repeat the procedure with the words below.

force	thorn	score	shore
hoarse	roar		

If... students hesitate while reading a word,
then... model blending each word without pausing between sounds (Routine Cards 1, 5).

On Their Own Use Worktext p. 39 and the Word List for additional practice. Challenge students to use each word in a sentence.

Mini-Lesson 3 R-Controlled Vowel /ėr/ *er, ir, ur*

Remind students that...

- Consonants and vowels may join together to spell a new sound.
- An *r*-controlled vowel sound is the sound of a vowel immediately followed by *r* in the same syllable.
- Many words contain the sound /ėr/ spelled *er, ir, ur*.

Word List

certain	skirt	curb
herd	third	hurt

Guide Practice

Have students practice reading and spelling words with the sound /êr/. Write *verb, stir,* and *curl.* Run your hand under each word as you have students blend it with you several times. Look carefully at how these words are spelled. What letter combinations spell the sound /êr/ in

these words? If students have difficulty identifying *er, ir,* and *ur,* point to those letters as you say /êr/ several times. Remember, the sound /êr/ can be spelled *er, ir,* or *ur.*

Repeat the process and model sound-by-sound blending (Routine Card 1) as students practice reading the words below. Encourage discussion of each word's meaning.

dessert	prefer	birth	thirsty
blurt	burns		

If... students have difficulty reading a word,
then... run your finger along *er, ir,* or *ur* as you say /êr/ with them.

On Their Own For more practice, have students complete Worktext p. 40 and use letter tiles to spell and read the Word List. Invite questions about each word's meaning.

Vowel Digraphs (Long *e* and *a*)

Objectives:
- Teach concept of vowel digraphs.
- Introduce /ē/ spelled *ee, ei.*
- Introduce /ē/ spelled *ea.*
- Introduce /ā/ spelled *ai, ay.*

MATERIALS
- Worktext pp. 41–43
- Routine Cards 1, 2, 3
- Letter tiles

Set the scene Help students remember that the same vowel sound can be spelled in different ways. Explain that in this lesson they will learn to read words with the **long *e*** sound spelled *ee, ei,* and *ea* and the **long *a*** sound spelled *ai* and *ay.*

Routine **1. Connect Sound to Spelling** Write and say *she, dusty,* and *scene.* What sound do you hear in all three words? (long *e*, /ē/) Which letter stands for the long *e* sound in each word? (*e* in *she, y* in *dusty, e_e* in *scene*) Today you will learn to read words with the long *e* sound spelled *ee* and *ei.*

2. Model and Give Examples Write *ee.* The sound /ē/ can be spelled *ee* as in the word *steep.* Have students repeat /ē/ several times as you point to *ee.* Repeat with *ei* as in the word *ceiling.*

3. Model Blending Write *steep.* In this word, the letters *ee* (point to them) spell the long *e* sound, /ē/. Run your hand under *steep* as you blend each sound: /s//t//ē//p/, *steep.* Have students blend the word with you. Follow this procedure to model *keen* and *ceiling.* Remember, when you see the spelling *ee* or *ei* in a word, try /ē/. Develop word meaning by asking questions (for example, *Climbing a steep hill can be difficult. Why? What other things can be steep? If you have keen eyesight, is that good? Where do you find a ceiling?*).

Mini-Lesson 1 — Long *e* (spelled *ee, ei*)

Remind students that...
- Long vowel sounds can be spelled different ways.
- Many words contain /ē/ spelled *ee* or *ei.*

Word List

between	sleeve
peel	neither
seen	seize

Guide Practice
Use the routine above to help students blend words with **long *e*** spelled *ee* and *ei.* Write *breeze.* Listen as I blend this word. Point to each spelling as you say its sound: /b//r//ē//z/, *breeze.* Have students blend with you. Repeat the process to introduce the remaining *ee* and *ei* words. Point to all the words again. Which letters spell the long *e* sound in these words? (*ee* and *ei*) Encourage students to discuss the meaning(s) of each word. Have students take turns using each word in a sentence.

breeze	fleet	glee	either	receive

If... students have trouble reading words,
then... have them think about the sound for each spelling they say. Have them say the sounds in their heads before reading the word aloud as you run your hand under it.

On Their Own For more practice, have students complete Worktext p. 41. In addition, help students use letter tiles to spell and read the words on the Word List. Discuss their meanings.

Mini-Lesson 2 — Long *e* (spelled *ea*)

Remind students that...
- Long vowel sounds can be spelled different ways.
- Many words contain /ē/ spelled *ea*.

Word List
appeal	feature
cheat	leap
eagle	plead

Guide Practice
Use sound-by-sound and word-by-word blending strategies (Routine Cards 1, 2) to help students connect /ē/ with *ea* and to blend **long e** words. Write and say *clean.* Use it in a sentence. What letters spell the long *e* sound you hear in the word *clean?* Point to or circle *ea.* Have students blend the word with you: /k//l//ē//n/, *clean.*

Repeat the procedure with the words below. Discuss the meaning of each word with students. Have students work in pairs to make up a sentence that uses each word.

feast   reach   treat   season   wheat

If... students cannot read a word,
then... try vowel-first blending. Point to the letters *ea* and exaggerate the /ē/ sound before you blend the whole word (Routine Card 3). Then add the other sound-spellings and have students say the sounds without pausing between them.

On Their Own See Worktext p. 42 and the Word List for additional practice with words with long *e* spelled *ea.* Help students spell each word with letter tiles.

Mini-Lesson 3 — Long *a* (spelled *ai, ay*)

Remind students that...
- Long vowel sounds can be spelled different ways.
- Many words contain /ā/ spelled *ai* or *ay.*

Word List
raisin	away
snail	decay
strain	holiday

Guide Practice
Remind students that they have learned several ways to spell the sound /ā/. Write and say *acorn* and *vase.* What letters stand for /ā/ in these words? (*Acorn* has /ā/ spelled *a; vase* has /ā/ spelled *a_e.*) Today you will learn to spell and read words with the **long a** sound spelled *ai* and *ay.*

Write *afraid, braid,* and *claim.* Point to or circle the letters *ai* in each word. When you see *ai* in a word, try the sound /ā/. Blend each word with students. Point to the letters as you say their sounds. Then repeat the procedure to introduce long *a* spelled *ay* in the remaining words. Discuss the meaning of each word.

afraid   braid   claim   display
essay   spray

If... students cannot read a word,
then... model how to blend the sounds slowly at first and then quickly as you touch under the letter(s).

On Their Own For additional practice, have students complete Worktext p. 43 and practice reading and spelling the Word List words.

Vowel Digraphs (Long *o* and *i*)

Objectives:

- Introduce /ō/ spelled *ow* and *ou*.
- Introduce /ō/ spelled *oa* and *oe*.
- Introduce /ī/ spelled *ie, igh*.

MATERIALS

- Worktext pp. 44–46
- Routine Cards 2, 5
- Letter tiles

Set the scene Remind students that long vowel sounds can be spelled different ways. You have learned to spell /ō/ with the letters *o* and *o_e,* and you have learned to spell /ī/ with the letters *i* and *i_e.* In this lesson, we'll spell **long *o*** and ***i*** sounds in other ways.

Routine **1. Connect Sound to Spelling** Write *choke* and *twine.* Have students say the words with you, and then ask volunteers to use each word in a sentence. What are the vowel sounds in these words? (/ō/, /ī/) Today we will learn to spell and read words with the sounds /ō/ and /ī/ spelled in different ways.

2. Model and Give Examples Write and say *below.* Point to *ow.* The letters *ow* spell the sound /ō/ in this word. Have students say /ō/ as you point to *ow.* Then ask students to tell you the meaning of *below.* Write *shoulder* and point to *ou.* These letters spell /ō/ in this word. Invite students to complete this sentence: My shoulders are below my _____. (head)

3. Model Blending Write *stow.* This word has the letters *ow* for the long *o* sound, /ō/. This is how I blend this word. Point to each spelling as you say its sound. Then run your hand under *stow* as you blend the whole word: /s//t//ō/, *stow.*

Mini-Lesson 1 Long o (spelled *ow, ou*)

Remind students that...

- Long vowel sounds can be spelled different ways.
- Many words contain the sound /ō/ spelled *ow.*
- Some words contain the sound /ō/ spelled *ou.*

Word List

throw	boulder
glow	shoulder
grown	dough
shadow	thorough

Guide Practice

Help students read words with the **long *o*** sound spelled ***ow*** and ***ou.*** Write *elbow.* Have students say /ō/ with you as you point to the letters *ow.* This is how I blend *elbow.* Run your hand under *elbow* as you blend: /e//l//b//ō/. Have students blend with you. Ask a volunteer to use *elbow* in a sentence.

Repeat with the long *o* sound spelled *ou,* using the word *though.* Have students say /ō/ with you as you point to the letters *ou.* Continue guiding practice with the following words.

blown	slower	owner
fellow	although	poultry

If... students mispronounce *ow* and *ou,*
then... have them say /ō/ as you touch under the letters. Return to the word later in the practice.

On Their Own For additional practice, have students complete Worktext p. 44. Have students use letter tiles to build and read words on the Word List.

Mini-Lesson 2 — Long o (spelled *oa* and *oe*)

Remind students that…
- Long vowel sounds can be spelled different ways.
- Many words contain the sound /ō/ spelled **oa.**
- Some words contain the sound /ō/ spelled **oe.**

Word List

boast	oboe
coach	toe
toast	goes
hoax	hoe

Guide Practice

Write *coast* and have students say it aloud with you. Today we will learn that the letters **oa** and **oe** can also spell the sound /ō/. Have students say /ō/ as you point to *oa.* Run your hand under each letter as you blend the whole word: /k//ō//s//t/, *coast.*

Write *goes.* Have students say /ō/ as you point to the letters *oe.* Blend the whole word: /g//ō//z/, *goes.* Prompt students to use *goes* and *coast* in a single sentence, such as "This road goes to the coast."

Repeat the procedure to guide practice with the words below.

float	soak	throat
foe	doe	flamingoes

If… students hesitate while reading a word,

then… use the fluent reading routine (Routine Card 5) to help them read each word smoothly.

On Their Own See Worktext p. 45 and the Word List for additional practice. Ask students to take turns reading a word, describing its meaning, and using it in a sentence.

Mini-Lesson 3 — Long i (spelled *ie, igh*)

Remind students that…
- Long vowel sounds can be spelled different ways.
- Many words contain the sound /ī/ spelled **ie** and **igh.**

Word List

supplies	delight
untie	highway
fright	tighten

Guide Practice

Remind students that the **long i** sound has different spellings. Write and say *hi, my,* and *nice.* Point to the sound /ī/ and its spelling in each word. Today we're going to learn to spell the sound /ī/ with *ie* and *igh*. Write *lie.* Have students say /i/ as you point to *ie.* Let's blend this word together: /l//ī/, *lie.* Repeat this procedure to model blending /ī/ spelled *igh* as in *bright.* Ask students to tell what *bright* means ("lit-up," "smart"). Continue the process to blend and define each word below.

pie	tries	upright	knight

If… students have difficulty recognizing /ī/ spelled *ie* and *igh,*

then… draw a circle around the letters *ie* or *igh* in the word and say the long *i* sound. Model blending each word as you point to each sound-spelling.

On Their Own For additional practice, use Worktext p. 46. Use Routine Card 2 to help students blend words from the Word List.

Phonics and Decoding Lesson 16
More Vowel Sounds

Objectives:
- Introduce /e/ spelled *ea.*
- Introduce /u̇/ spelled *oo, ou.*
- Introduce /ē/ spelled *ie, ey.*

MATERIALS
- Worktext pp. 47–49
- Routine Cards 2, 8
- Letter tiles

Set the scene Remind students that vowel sounds can be spelled differently. You learned to spell the /ē/ sound with the letters *ea* or *ee.* Today we'll learn to read words with the **short e** sound spelled *ea,* the /u̇/ sound spelled *oo* and *ou,* and the **long e** sound spelled *ie* and *ey.*

Routine

1. Connect Sound to Spelling Write and say *stream* and *squeak* several times. What is the vowel sound in these words? (/ē/) The long *e* is spelled *ea* in these words. Today you will learn words in which *ea* spells the short *e* sound, /e/.

2. Model and Give Examples Write *bedspread* and say it several times. In this word, the /e/ sound is spelled with *e* in the first syllable, *bed,* and with *ea* in the second syllable, *spread.* Have students say /e/ several times as you point to *ea.* Ask them to tell you what *bedspread* means.

3. Model Blending Write *bread.* This word has the letters *ea.* Point to them. They spell the /e/ sound. This is how I blend this word. Point to each spelling as you say its sound. Then run your hand under *bread* as you blend the whole word: /b//r//e//d/, *bread.* Have students say the word several times without pausing between sounds. Use Routine Card 2 to model blending *steady* and *ready.*

Mini-Lesson 1 Sound /e/ spelled *ea*

Remind students that...
- The same vowel sound can be spelled in different ways.
- Many words contain the short *e* sound /e/ spelled *ea.*

Word List

weather	sweaty
instead	thread
unsteady	

Guide Practice
Help students read words with the **/e/** sound spelled *ea.* Write *ahead* and ask students to say it with you. Notice the letters *ea.* What sound do they stand for in *ahead?* (/e/) Listen to how I blend this word. Run your hand under each letter as you blend the whole word: /ə//h//e//d/, *ahead.* Ask a volunteer to use the word in a sentence. Repeat this process with the other words below.

ahead	breath	pleasant
meant	health	

If... students cannot read a word,
then... use whole-word blending (Routine Card 2). Say each word, use it in a sentence, and then have students repeat the word with you.

On Their Own For additional practice, use the Word List and Worktext p. 47. Help students use letter tiles to spell each word, and then have them use each word in a sentence.

Mini-Lesson 2 — Sound /ù/ spelled *oo* and *ou*

Remind students that...
- Vowel sounds can be spelled different ways.
- Many words contain the sound /ù/ spelled *oo*.
- A few words contain the sound /ù/ spelled *ou*.

Word List

crook	shook
understood	would
wool	could

Guide Practice

The letters *oo* can spell the sound /ù/, as in *look*. Write *look*. Have students say /ù/ as you point to *oo*. Listen as I blend this word. Point to each letter as you say the sound. Then run your hand under *look* as you blend the whole word: /l//ù//k/, *look*.

Only a few English words have the sound /ù/ spelled *ou*. Write *should*. Have students say /ù/ as you point to *ou*. Then blend the whole word. Repeat the procedure with the words below.

book   roof   hoof   overtook   wooden

Write *wood* and *would* and ask how their meanings are different.

If... students have difficulty making the /ù/ sound,
then... have them say each word silently before reading it aloud.

On Their Own See Worktext p. 48 and the Word List for additional practice. Have students take turns using each word in a sentence.

Mini-Lesson 3 — Sound /ē/ spelled *ie, ey*

Remind students that...
- Vowel sounds can be spelled different ways.
- Many words contain the long *e* sound spelled *ie, ey*.

Word List

relieve	journey
brief	keys
shield	baloney

Guide Practice

Remind students that the **long *e*** sound has different spellings. Write *we, ceiling, treat,* and *deep*. Point to *e, ei, ea,* and *ee* in the words as you say each word several times. Today we will learn to read words that have /ē/ spelled *ie* and *ey*. Write *field*. Have students say /ē/ as you point to *ie*. Point to each sound-spelling as you blend the word: /f//ē//l//d/, *field*. Have students blend the whole word and then use it in a sentence.

Repeat this procedure for *ey* in the word *chimney*. Continue the process to help students blend and use the remaining words below.

believe   achieve   belief   jockey   donkey

If... students cannot read the words,
then... exaggerate the /ē/ sound as you model blending each word several times.

On Their Own For additional practice, use Worktext p. 49 and the Word List.

Vowel Patterns with /ü/

Objectives:
- Introduce /ü/ spelled *oo.*
- Introduce /ü/ spelled *ew, ou.*
- Introduce /ü/ spelled *ue, ui.*

MATERIALS
- Worktext pp. 50–52
- Routine Cards 1, 5
- Letter tiles

Set the scene Remind students that the same vowel sound can be spelled in different ways. You have learned that the letters *i, ie,* and *igh* can spell the sound /ī/. Now we'll learn that the sound /ü/ can be spelled with *oo, ew, ou, ue,* and *ui.*

Routine **1. Connect Sound to Spelling** Write *twine, lie,* and *might.* Have students say the words with you. What do you know about the /ī/ sound in these words? (It is spelled *i_e* in *twine, ie* in *lie,* and *igh* in *might.*) The /ī/ sound can be spelled in many ways. Today we will learn to spell the /ü/ sound, as in *balloon,* in many ways, with the letters *oo, ew, ou, ue,* and *ui.*

2. Model and Give Examples Write *spoon* and point to the letters *oo.* The sound /ü/ can be spelled *oo.* Have students say /ü/ several times as you point to *oo.* The letters *oo* spell the sound /ü/ as in *spoon, moon,* and *noon.*

3. Model Blending Blend *spoon.* Point to each spelling as you say its sound. Then run your hand under *spoon* as you blend the whole word: /s//p//ü//n/, *spoon.* Ask a volunteer to use *spoon* in a sentence. Follow this procedure to model blending and defining *balloon.*

Mini-Lesson 1 Sound /ü/ spelled *oo*

Remind students that...
- Vowel sounds can be spelled different ways.
- Many words contain the sound /ü/ spelled *oo.*

Word List
choose	moose
kangaroo	soon
school	snooze

Guide Practice
Write *broom.* In this word, the letters *oo* spell /ü/. Have students say /ü/ several times with you as you point to the letters *oo.* Listen to how I blend this word. Run your hand under *broom* as you blend the whole word: /b//r//ü//m/, *broom.* Have students say it with you, and then ask a volunteer to use *broom* in a sentence. Continue this process with the other words below. Talk about the meaning of each word. As a group, create example sentences for each word.

gloomy	scoop	shoot	drool
loose	boomerang		

If... students cannot read a word,
then... use Routine Card 1 to help them practice blending sounds into a word.

On Their Own For additional practice, use the Word List and Worktext p. 50. Model blending each word and then ask students to blend it with you.

Mini-Lesson 2 — Sound /ü/ spelled *ew*, *ou*

Remind students that...
- Different spellings can represent the same vowel sound.
- Many words contain the sound **/ü/** spelled **ew.**
- Some words contain the sound **/ü/** spelled **ou.**

Word List

blew	group
drew	you
knew	cougar

Guide Practice
Remind students that **/ü/** can be spelled *oo,* as in *spoon.* Today we will learn that **ew** and **ou** can also spell /ü/.

Write *stew.* Have students say /ü/ as you point to *ew.* The letters *ew* spell the sound /ü/ in *stew.* Listen as I blend this word. Point to each spelling as you say the sound. Then run your hand under *stew* as you blend the whole word: /s//t//ü/, *stew.*

Write *soup.* Point to *ou* and have students say /ü/. In the word *soup,* the letters *ou* spell /ü/. Listen as I blend this word: /s//ü//p/. Have students tell you how the meanings of *stew* and *soup* are similar and different.

Repeat the blending procedure with the remaining words. Discuss the meaning of each word.

chew	grew	tour	coupon

If... students have difficulty reading words,
then... use Routine Card 5 to help them develop fluency.

On Their Own See Worktext p. 51 and the Word List for additional practice. Have volunteers use each word in a sentence.

Mini-Lesson 3 — Sound /ü/ spelled *ue*, *ui*

Remind students that...
- Many vowel sounds can be spelled in several ways.
- Some words contain the sound **/ü/** spelled **ue** and **ui.**

Word List

unglued	bruise
true	recruit
clue	suit

Guide Practice
Remind students that **/ü/** has different spellings. Write *cartoon* and *renew.* Point to *oo* and *ew* as you say /ü/. Today we're going to learn that **ue** and **ui** can spell this sound.

Write *statue.* Have students say /ü/ as you point to *ue.* Run your hand under *statue* as students join you in blending the whole word several times: /s//t//a//ch//ü/, *statue.* Ask volunteers to use the word *statue* in a sentence.

Follow this procedure for *ui* in the word *suit.* Then continue the process to have students blend each word below and use it in a sentence.

blue	overdue	fruit	juice

If... students have difficulty spelling /ü/ with *ue* and *ui,*
then... exaggerate the /ü/ sound as you model blending each word several times.

On Their Own For additional practice, use Worktext p. 52. Have students use letter tiles to build the Word List words. Help them use each word in a sentence.

Phonics and Decoding Lesson 18
Vowel Diphthongs

Objectives:
- Introduce **/ou/** spelled *ou.*
- Introduce **/ou/** spelled *ow.*
- Introduce **/oi/** spelled *oi, oy.*

MATERIALS
- Worktext pp. 53–55
- Routine Cards 2, 5
- Letter tiles

Set the scene Remind students that vowel sounds can be spelled in a number of different ways. You know that the sounds /ü/ and /ů/ can be spelled with the letters *oo.* In this lesson, we will learn words with the **/ou/** sound spelled *ou* and *ow* and the **/oi/** sound spelled *oi* and *oy.*

Routine **1. Connect Sound to Spelling** Write *balloon* and *notebook* and say them aloud several times. What sounds do the letters *oo* spell in these words? (In *balloon,* they spell /ü/. In *notebook,* they spell /ů/.) Today we'll learn words with the sound /ou/ spelled *ou,* as in *loud,* and *ow,* as in *how.* We'll also learn to spell the sound /oi/ with the letter combinations *oi* and *oy.*

2. Model and Give Examples Write *pounce.* We can use the letters *ou* to spell the sound /ou/. Have students say /ou/ as you point to *ou.* The letters *ou* spell the sound /ou/ in words like *pounce, amount,* and *round.*

3. Model Blending Write *slouch.* The letters *ou* spell the sound /ou/ in this word. Point to the letters *ou* and have students say /ou/ with you. Listen to me blend this word: /s//l//ou//ch/, *slouch.* Run your hand under *slouch* as you blend the whole word several times. Then discuss the word's meaning. What does it mean to slouch?

Mini-Lesson 1 — Vowel Diphthong /ou/ *ou*

Remind students that...
- A vowel sound can be spelled in more than one way.
- The sound **/ou/** can be spelled *ou.*

Word List

aloud	found
hound	announce
out	

Guide Practice

Help students recognize and blend /ou/ spelled *ou.* Write *pounds.* Point to the letters *ou.* The letters *ou* spell the sound /ou/. Let's blend the word together. Use Routine Card 2 to practice blending. As you run your hand under *pounds,* say each sound slowly: /p//ou//n//d//z/. After blending the word several times, ask students to take turns using it in a sentence.

Repeat the procedure with the words below.

rebound	crouch	doubt	southwest

If... students have difficulty reading the words, **then...** use Routine Card 5 to build fluency skills.

On Their Own For additional practice, see Worktext p. 53. Have students use letter tiles to build and define words on the Word List.

 **Mini-Lesson 2** **Vowel Diphthong /ou/ *ow***

Remind students that...
- Sounds can often be spelled in more than one way.
- Many words contain the sound **/ou/** spelled ***ow.***

Word List

coward	however
crowd	chow
gown	

Guide Practice

Write *power.* Today we will learn that the letters ***ow*** can spell the sound **/ou/.** Have students say /ou/ as you point to ***ow.*** To blend the word, point to each letter as you say its sound: /p//ou//ər/. Then run your hand under *power* as you blend the whole word. Ask a volunteer to use *power* in a sentence. Be sure that students know the meaning of each word.

Repeat this procedure to guide practice with the words below.

downward	shower	towel	vow	tower

If... students mispronounce *ow* as /ō/ in a word, **then...** model the correct pronunciation, exaggerating the position of your lips as you say /ou/. Return to the word later in the practice.

On Their Own See Worktext p. 54 and the Word List for additional practice. Challenge students to use two or more of the Word List words in a single sentence.

Mini-Lesson 3 **Vowel Diphthong /oi/ *oi, oy***

Remind students that...
- They can use two-letter combinations to spell some vowel sounds.
- The letter combinations *oi* and *oy* spell **/oi/.**

Word List

coil	enjoy
choice	annoy
poise	oyster

Guide Practice

Write *spoil.* Today we will learn that the letters ***oi*** and ***oy*** spell the sound **/oi/.** Have students say /oi/ several times as you point to the letters in *spoil.* This is how I blend this word. Point to each letter as you say its sound. Then run your hand under *spoil* as you blend the whole word: /s//p// oi//l/. Have students blend the word with you several times. Ask them to tell you in their own words what *spoil* means.

Repeat the procedure with the word *loyal* to introduce /oi/ spelled *oy.* Continue guiding practice with the words below, blending them and asking students what they mean.

disappoint	toil	avoid	voyage	royal

If... students have difficulty reading the words, **then...** use Routine Card 5 to help them build fluency.

On Their Own For additional practice with /oi/ spelled *oi* and *oy,* use Worktext p. 55 and the Word List.

Vowel Patterns with /ȯ/

Objectives:
- Introduce /ȯ/ spelled **a, al.**
- Introduce /ȯ/ spelled **au, aw.**
- Introduce /ȯ/ spelled **augh, ough.**

MATERIALS
- Worktext pp. 56–58
- Routine Cards 2, 5
- Letter tiles

Set the scene Remind students that vowel sounds have various spellings. You know that /ā/ can be spelled with the letters *ai*, as in *rain*, and the letters *ay*, as in *say*. Today we will learn that the sound /ȯ/ can be spelled in many ways.

Routine

1. Connect Sound to Spelling Write *chain* and *play*. Point to the vowels in each word. In *chain*, *ai* spells /ā/. In *play*, *ay* spells /ā/. The sound /ȯ/, as in the words *daughter* and *claw*, can be spelled with the letter *a* and with the letter combinations *al, au, aw, augh*, and *ough*.

2. Model and Give Examples Write *stall* and point to the letter *a*. The letter *a* can spell the sound /ȯ/. Have students say /ȯ/ as you point to *a*. Write *chalk* and repeat this procedure for *al* as in *chalk*.

3. Model Blending Write *hallway*. Point to the *a* in *hall*. In this part of the word, the letter *a* spells the /ȯ/ sound. Listen as I blend this word. Point to each spelling as you say its sound. Then run your hand under *hallway* as you blend the whole word: /h//ȯ//l//w//ā/, *hallway*. Who can use the word *hallway* in a sentence? Invite volunteers to share their sentences. Follow the same procedure to model blending *stalk*, and have students use it in a sentence, as in the *stalk* of a plant.

Mini-Lesson 1 Sound /ȯ/ spelled *a, al*

Remind students that...
- Vowel sounds can be spelled different ways.
- Some words contain the sound /ȯ/ spelled **a, al.**

Word List
small	scald
halt	alternate
walk	

Guide Practice
Write *halt*. Have students say /ȯ/ several times with you as you point to the *a*. Let's blend this word together. Run your hand under each sound-spelling in *halt* as you say its sound: /h//ȯ//l//t/, *halt*. Ask students to give you examples of times they might shout "Halt!"

Follow this procedure to model blending words with /ȯ/ spelled *all*, as in *ball* and *fall*, and to blend the words below. For each word, discuss the meaning and have students use it in a sentence.

snowfall	small	crosswalk
talk	salty	

If... students cannot read a word,
then... use whole-word blending (Routine Card 2) and return to the word later in the practice.

On Their Own For more practice, use Worktext p. 56 and the Word List. Ask students to identify the /ȯ/ sound in each word as they use letter tiles to spell it out.

Mini-Lesson 2 — Sound /ȯ/ spelled *au, aw*

Remind students that...
- Different letter combinations can represent the same vowel sound.
- Some words contain the sound **/ȯ/** spelled *au, aw.*

Word List

because	scrawl
fault	crawl
autograph	saw

Guide Practice

Tell students that today they will learn words in which *au* and *aw* spell the sound **/ȯ/**. Write *author.* The letters *au* spell /ȯ/ in *author.* Listen as I blend this word. Point to each spelling as you say the sound. Run your hand under *author* as you blend the whole word: /ȯ//th//ər/, *author.* Have students say the word and then tell you what it means.

Sometimes the letters *aw* spell /ȯ/, as in *drawl* and *bawl.* Write these words, blend them with students, and discuss the meaning of the words. Continue to guide practice with the words below.

caused	**applause**	**sauce**	**bawl**
awful	**shawl**		

If... students have difficulty reading words,
then... use Routine Card 5 to help them gain fluency with *au* and *aw* spellings.

On Their Own Use Worktext p. 57 and the Word List for additional practice.

Mini-Lesson 3 — Sound /ȯ/ spelled *augh, ough*

Remind students that...
- Some vowel sounds have many different spellings.
- Some words contain the sound **/ȯ/** spelled **augh, ough.**

Word List

daughter	brought
taught	fought
sought	

Guide Practice

Write *stall* and *brawn.* Point to the *a* and then the *aw* and say /ȯ/. You've been learning words with the **/ȯ/** sound. Today we will learn that this sound can be spelled **augh** and **ough.** Write *taught.* Run your hand under *taught* as you have students blend the whole word several times: /t//ȯ//t/, *taught.* Ask students to tell you something they have taught to another person.

Repeat this procedure for *ough* in the word *bought.* Ask students to name something they wish they had bought. Continue having students blend and discuss the meanings of the words below.

caught	**haughty**	**ought**	**thought**

If... students misread a word,
then... use Routine Card 2 to have students blend the word and pronounce it several times.

On Their Own For additional practice, use Worktext p. 58, and have students use letter tiles to build words from the Word List.

Schwa Sound and Silent Letters

Objectives:
- Review the concept of the schwa sound /ə/.
- Review the concept of silent letters.
- Recognize words with the schwa sound in first and second syllables.
- Introduce words with /n/ kn.

MATERIALS
- Worktext pp. 59–61
- Routine Cards 1, 6, 8
- Letter tiles

Set the scene Remind students that different letters can spell the same vowel sound. You know that the long *o* sound can be spelled *ow* as in *bowl*, *ough* as in *dough*, *oa* as in *goat*, and *oe* as in *goes*. Today we'll learn spellings of the schwa sound, /ə/. We'll also learn the sound /n/ spelled **kn**.

Routine **1. Connect Sound to Spelling** Remind students that they know many words with two syllables. Write *alert* and *album*. These words have two syllables: *a•lert*, *al•bum*.

2. Model and Give Examples Point to *alert*. When I say *alert*, I stress the second syllable: *a•lert*. Repeat *alert* and *album*, emphasizing the different stresses. Point to the *a* in *alert*. I see the letter *a*, but when I say *alert*, I don't hear the /a/ sound or the /ā/ sound. I hear /ə/: *a•lert*. This /ə/ is the schwa sound. The schwa sound occurs in an unstressed syllable.

3. Model Blending Point to *alert* again. In *alert*, *a* spells /ə/. Model blending the whole word: /ə//l//ėr//t/. Ask students to define *alert*. Then write *occur*. Have students read the word with you. Show students that in *occur*, *o* spells the schwa sound. Different letters can spell the schwa sound in unstressed syllables.

Mini-Lesson 1 — Sound /ə/ in First Syllable

Remind students that...
- The vowel sound in an unaccented syllable often is /ə/, the schwa sound.
- The sound /ə/ can be spelled different ways.
- Many words contain the schwa sound in the first syllable.

Word List
career	mistake
police	tonight
suggest	percent

Guide Practice
Write *parade* and read the word aloud. This word has two syllables, *pa* and *rade*. Say the word with me and listen for the stressed syllable: *pa•rade*. We stress the second syllable, *rade*. The first syllable has the schwa sound, /ə/. In *parade*, *a* spells the schwa sound. Ask a volunteer to use *parade* in a sentence.

Repeat the procedure to help students identify the schwa sound and the letter that spells it in each word below. Have a volunteer use each word in a sentence.

correct	herself	divide
suspend	salute	

If... students cannot read a word,
then... use Routine Card 1 to blend the word sound by sound with students. Return to the word later in the practice.

On Their Own For additional practice, see Worktext p. 59. Use letter tiles to help students build words from the Word List. Have students point to each letter that represents the schwa sound and then use each word in a sentence.

Mini-Lesson 2 — Sound /ə/ in Second Syllable

Remind students that...
- Different letters can spell vowel sounds, including /ə/.
- The vowel sound in an unaccented syllable may be /ə/, the schwa sound.
- Many words contain the schwa sound in the second syllable.

Word List

equal	hammer
legend	anchor
picture	nation

Guide Practice

Tell students that in this lesson they will learn some words with the schwa sound, /ə/, in the second syllable. Write *backward*. *Backward* has two syllables: *back* and *ward*. Let's say the word together and listen for the stressed syllable: **back**•*ward*. We stress the first syllable, *back*. The *a* in the second syllable (point to the second *a*), stands for the schwa sound, /ə/. Blend the whole word as you run your hand under it. Invite a volunteer to demonstrate the meaning of *backward*.

Write the words below and repeat the procedure to help students read them. Point to the letters in the unaccented syllables that spell the schwa sound.

action	person	glimmer
restful	muffin	

If... students cannot read a word,

then... help them break the words into syllables (Routine Card 6), blend the word with them, and then define the word.

On Their Own See Worktext p. 60 and the Word List for additional practice. Ask students to point to the /ə/ sound in each word.

Mini-Lesson 3 — Silent Letter /n/ Spelled *kn*

Remind students that...
- Sounds can be spelled different ways.
- Some letters can be silent.
- Many words contain the sound /n/ spelled *kn*.

Word List

kneel	knitting
unknown	knapsack
knight	

Guide Practice

Write *knock* and point to the letters **kn.** These letters spell the sound /n/. Let's blend this word. Run your hand under *knock* and say each sound slowly: /n//o//k/. Say the word with me: *knock.* The *k* in *knock* is silent. Ask a volunteer to use *knock* in a sentence or to demonstrate what the word means.

Repeat the procedure to blend, read, and have students define the words below.

knives	knob	knack	knead	knuckle

If... students have difficulty reading words that begin with *kn.*

then... remind them that *k* is silent. Have students blend the words with you several times. Compare the meanings of *know* and *no, knight* and *night,* and *knead* and *need.*

On Their Own For additional practice, use the Word List and Worktext p. 61.

Phonics and Decoding Lesson 21
More Silent Letters

Objectives:
- Review the concept of silent letters.
- Introduce **/r/** spelled **wr.**
- Introduce **/m/** spelled **mb.**
- Introduce words with **/n/** **gn** and **/s/ st.**

MATERIALS
- Worktext pp. 62–64
- Routine Cards 1, 2, 8
- Letter tiles

Set the scene Tell students that not every letter in every word always stands for a sound. Today we'll learn to read words with silent letters. For instance, we'll read words that begin with the letters **wr,** like *wrist.* In these words, the *w* is silent.

Routine **1. Connect Sound to Spelling** Write *right* and *write.* The sounds in these words are /r//ī//t/. Point to *right.* We learned that the sound /ī/ can be spelled *igh: right.* Point to *write.* In the word *write,* the sound **/r/** is spelled *wr.*

2. Model and Give Examples Write *ring* and have a volunteer use *ring* in a sentence. Then write *wring.* This word sounds like *ring,* but it has a different meaning. *Wring* means "twist." Have a volunteer demonstrate wringing water from an imaginary towel. The letters *wr* spell the sound /r/ at the beginning of words like *write, wring, wrong,* and *wreck.* The *w* in these words is silent.

3. Model Blending Write *wreath.* In this word, the letters *wr* spell /r/. Here is how I blend *wreath:* /r//ē//th/. Run your hand under *wreath* as you blend the whole word. Repeat the procedure to model blending *wrench.* When you see the spelling *wr* at the beginning of a word, the *w* is silent.

Mini-Lesson 1 — Silent Letter /r/ Spelled *wr*

Remind students that...
- The same sound can often be spelled different ways.
- Some letters in a word can be silent.
- Some words contain the sound **/r/** spelled **wr.**

Word List

wrinkled	written
wrapper	shipwreck
wren	

Guide Practice
Write *wr.* The letters *wr* at the beginning of a word spell the sound **/r/.** Write *wrath* and say /r/ several times as you point to *wr.* Use Routine Card 1 to blend the word, writing *wr* for the /r/ sound at the beginning of the word. Give students a sample sentence, such as "I was filled with wrath when I saw the broken vase," and ask them to tell you what *wrath* means. Repeat this procedure with the words below.

wreck	wristwatch	wrist
wrestle	wrong	

If... students mispronounce a word,
then... use Routine Card 2 to practice blending the whole word with *wr.* Return to the word later in the practice.

On Their Own See Worktext p. 62 and the Word List for additional practice. Point out that *shipwreck* is a compound word.

Mini-Lesson 2 — Silent Letter /m/ Spelled *mb*

Remind students that...
- Sounds can be spelled with different letter combinations.
- In some spellings, letters can be silent.
- Some words contain the sound **/m/** spelled **mb.**

Word List

comb	beachcomber
lamb	climber
numb	

Guide Practice

Point out that the letter *m* spells **/m/** in words like *lime* and *limber.* Then write *limb.* Ask students to describe the limb of a tree. The letters **mb** at the end of a word can spell the sound /m/. The *b* is silent. Circle the *mb* in *limb* and say /m/.

Write *climb.* The letters *mb* spell /m/ in *climb.* The *b* is silent. Listen as I blend the word. Point to each letter as you say its sound: /k//l//ī//m/. Have students blend the word with you; ask a volunteer to use *climb* in a sentence. Repeat this procedure to guide practice with the following words.

crumb	bomb	thumb	dumb

If... students have difficulty reading a word,
then... remind them that the *b* is silent. Have students blend the word with you several times.

On Their Own For additional practice, use Worktext p. 63. Have students use letter tiles to spell each word on the Word List. Invite volunteers to use each word in a sentence.

Mini-Lesson 3 — Silent Letters: /n/ spelled *gn* and /s/ spelled *st*

Remind students that...
- Sounds can have different spellings.
- Some letters can be silent.
- Some words contain the sound **/n/** spelled **gn** or the sound **/s/** spelled **st.**

Word List

gnaw	fasten
gnome	wrestle
gnat	moisten
foreign	

Guide Practice

Write *nest* and have students say it with you. In *nest,* the letter *n* spells the sound **/n/** and the letter *s* spells the sound **/s/.** Today we'll learn words with /n/ spelled **gn** and /s/ spelled **st.**

Write *assign* and circle *gn.* In this word, the letters *gn* spell /n/. The *g* is silent. Let's blend the word. Point to each letter as you blend the whole word: /ə//s//ī//n/. Have students tell you what *assign* means.

Repeat this procedure with *listen* to introduce and blend the sound /s/ spelled *st.* Continue guiding practice with the words below.

design	sign	reign	gnarled
castle	glisten	rustle	

If... students do not recognize a word,
then... blend the word with students several times.

On Their Own For additional practice, use Worktext p. 64 and the Word List. Have students blend the words and use them in sentences.

Phonics and Decoding Lesson 22
More Syllable Patterns

Objectives:

- Teach concept of syllable patterns.
- Introduce syllable pattern **C + le.**
- Introduce syllable pattern **VCCCV.**
- Introduce syllable pattern **CV/VC.**

MATERIALS

- Worktext pp. 65–67
- Routine Cards 2, 4
- Letter tiles

Set the scene Remind students that many words can be divided into smaller word parts, or syllables. Remember that you can use word parts to help you read many words. Today you will learn how to read words that contain three common syllable patterns.

Routine **1. Connect** Write *market.* Encourage students to look for meaningful parts when they read a long word. *What parts do you see in this word?* (It has two syllables, *mar, ket.*) Remind students that a syllable is a word part that contains a single vowel sound. Today we will learn to divide words that end with a consonant and the letters *le.* Write **C + le.**

2. Model and Give Examples Write and say *rumble.* How many syllables does *rumble* have? Cover *ble* and read the first syllable: *rum.* Cover *rum* and read the last syllable aloud: *ble.* Read the syllables one after the other: *rum, ble, rumble.* This word ends with a consonant (point to *b*) plus *le.*

3. Model Blending Write *gentle.* If the last syllable of a word ends in *le* and is preceded by a consonant (point to *t*), the consonant is usually the first letter of the last syllable. Help students identify the two syllables: *gen* and *tle.* Have students blend the syllables to say the word: *gen, tle, gentle.* Remember that the consonant and *le* form the final syllable. Guide students to think about the meanings of *market, rumble,* and *gentle* by asking questions (for example, *What would you see at a market? Why should you be gentle with a baby?*). Have students work together to use the words in sentences.

Mini-Lesson 1 — Syllable Pattern C + *le*

Remind students that...

- Some words can be broken into smaller word parts.
- A syllable is a word part that contains a single vowel sound.
- Many words contain the syllable pattern **C + le.**

Word List

castle	single
cycle	terrible
nuzzle	wrinkle

Guide Practice

Write and say *wiggle* and *stable.* These words end in the syllable pattern **C + le.** Ask students to identify the consonant that precedes *le* in each word. (*g* and *b*) When you see words that end with a consonant plus *le,* divide the word into syllables. The consonant and *le* form the final syllable. What is the last syllable in each word? (*gle* in *wiggle, ble* in *stable*). Read the words as you run your hand beneath the syllables: *wig, gle, wiggle; sta, ble, stable.*

Repeat the procedure with the words below. Ask pairs of students to discuss word meanings and think of a sentence that uses each word.

kettle	pebble	sparkle
struggle	vehicle	

If... students cannot read a word,

then... have them identify one syllable at a time as you cover the remaining syllable (Routine Card 4).

On Their Own Have students complete Worktext p. 65. In addition, use the Word List to give students more practice with C + *le* words.

T•50 Phonics and Decoding • Lesson 22

Copyright © Pearson Education, Inc., or its affiliates. All Rights Reserved.

Mini-Lesson 2 — Syllable Pattern VCCCV

Remind students that...
- Some words can be broken into smaller word parts.
- A syllable is a word part that contains a single vowel sound.
- Many words contain the syllable pattern **VCCCV**.

Word List

address	partner
extreme	pumpkin
orchard	sandwich

Guide Practice

Introduce students to words with the syllable pattern **VCCCV.** Write *children.* This word has three consonants in the middle. What are they? Point to *l,d,r.* If a word has three consonants in the middle, divide the word between the single consonant and the two consonants that work together to form a sound. Draw a line between *l* and *dr. Children* has two syllables. We divide *children* after *l*

because the letters *dr* stands for /dr/. Have students read the syllables with you: *chil, dren, children.*

Repeat the process with the remaining words. Have students identify the three consecutive consonants in each word and discuss the meaning of the word.

contract	inspect	kingdom
purchase	improve	

If... students cannot read a word,
then... use Routine Card 4 to help them identify its syllables. Use Routine Card 2 to blend the word's sounds.

On Their Own Use Worktext p. 66 and the Word List for additional practice. Have students work together to use each Word List word in a sentence.

Mini-Lesson 3 — Syllable Pattern CV/VC

Remind students that...
- Some words can be broken into smaller word parts.
- A syllable is a word part that contains a single vowel sound.
- Many words contain the syllable pattern **CV/VC**.

Word List

giant	lion
create	poem
dial	riot

Guide Practice

Use the routine on the previous page to help students read words with the syllable pattern **CV/VC.** You have learned to read words like *feet* when two vowels work together to make one sound, /ē/. But in some words, two vowels together stand for two separate sounds.

Write and say *trial.* The vowels *i* and *a* stand for two sounds. In a word with two vowels together, when each vowel spells a different sound, divide the word between the vowels. Draw a line between the *i* and *a.* Identify each syllable. Have students blend with you: *tri, al, trial.* Repeat the process to help students read the words below and identify the syllables in each one. Discuss word meanings with students.

diet	chaos	client	Noah

If... students cannot read a word,
then... break the word into syllables. Then stretch the vowel sound(s) in each syllable as you model blending the word.

On Their Own Give students more practice with the Word List words and Worktext p. 67.

Phonics and Decoding Lesson 23
Prefixes and Suffixes

Objectives:
- Teach concept of prefixes and suffixes.
- Introduce prefixes *re-, un-, dis-, pre-*.
- Introduce suffixes *-er, -or, -al, -less*.
- Introduce suffixes *-ly, -ful, -ness, -able*.

MATERIALS
- Worktext pp. 68–70
- Routine Cards 1, 4
- Letter tiles

Set the scene Remind students that they have learned to break many long words into smaller parts to make them easier to read. Today you will learn about prefixes and suffixes. **Prefixes** are word parts added to the beginning of a word. **Suffixes** are word parts added to the end of a word.

Routine **1. Connect** Connect today's lesson to students' knowledge of other word parts. Write and say *mission* and *softly*. How many syllables do you hear in each word? Draw a slash between the two syllables in each word: *mis/sion, soft/ly*. Many words end with the syllables *-sion* and *-ly*. Today we will learn to make and read words that begin with *re-* and *un-*.

2. Model and Give Examples Write and say *trace*. Add the word part *re-* to the beginning. *Re-* forms a special word part called a *prefix*. When I add these letters to *trace*, I change its meaning. The prefix *re-* means "again." *Retrace* means "to trace again." Repeat this procedure with the word *afraid* and the prefix *un-*. Explain that *un-* can mean "not" or "do the opposite of."

3. Model Blending Point to *retrace*. Look for words with the prefix *re-* as you read. The prefix *re-* and the base word *trace* make up the word *retrace*. To read this word, read the parts separately and then read them together: *re, trace, retrace*. Repeat the procedure with *unafraid*. Ask students to use each word in a sentence. Encourage them to brainstorm other words that begin with the prefixes *re-* and *un-* (for example, *recopy, review, unfair, unclear*).

Mini-Lesson 1 — Prefixes *re-, un-, dis-, pre-*

Remind students that...
- Many words can be broken into smaller parts.
- Prefixes are word parts that are added at the beginning of a word.
- Many words begin with the prefixes *re-, un-, dis-*, and *pre-*.

Word List
disconnect	recharge
disagree	redo
preview	unequal
preschool	undo

Guide Practice
Use the routine to help students make and read words with *re-, un-, dis-*, and *pre-*. Write each prefix. Many words begin with one of these prefixes. Under *re-*, write *retype*. Divide *re-* from *type* with a slash. Model blending the prefix with the base word: *re, type, retype*. The

prefix *re-* means "again." When we add *re-* to a word, it changes the meaning. What does *retype* mean? (to type again) Have students use *retype* in a sentence.

Use the same process to help students read the words below. Explain that *un-* means "not" or "do the opposite of," *dis-* means "not" or "opposite of," and *pre-* means "before."

dishonest	disobey	prehistoric
prejudge	resend	unsteady

If... students cannot read a word,
then... cover the prefix and help students blend the base word. Add the prefix and model reading the parts one after the other (Routine Cards 1, 4).

On Their Own For additional practice, have students complete Worktext p. 68 and practice reading the words on the Word List.

Mini-Lesson 2 — Suffixes -er, -or, -al, -less

Remind students that…
- Many words can be broken into smaller parts.
- Suffixes are word parts that are added at the end of a word.
- Many words end with the suffixes *-er, -or, -al,* and *-less.*

Word List

designer	classical
trumpeter	intentional
reviewer	careless
instructor	windowless

Guide Practice

Explain that a suffix is a word part that can be added at the end of a base word to make a new word. Today you will learn to make and read words with several common suffixes: *-er, -or, -al,* and *-less.*

Write this sentence: *The builder bought wood.* Underline *builder.* What parts do you see in this word? Identify *build* as the base word and *-er* as a suffix. The suffix *-er* means "one who." A builder is one who builds, or constructs. Have students practice reading the remaining words below with suffixes *-or, -al,* and *-less.* Explain their meanings. (The suffix *-or* means "one who," *-al* means "having characteristics of," and *-less* means "without.") Discuss word meanings with students.

inventor	emotional	professional
flavorless	joyless	

If… students hesitate while reading a word,
then… identify the suffix and blend the base word and suffix without pausing.

On Their Own Use Worktext p. 69 and the Word List for additional practice. Have students use letter tiles to build each word.

Mini-Lesson 3 — Suffixes -ly, -ful, -ness, -able

Remind students that…
- Many words can be broken into smaller parts.
- Suffixes are word parts that are added at the end of a word.
- Many words end with the suffixes *-ly, -ful, -ness,* and *-able.*

Word List

accidentally	kindness
largely	firmness
stressful	repairable
youthful	comfortable

Guide Practice

Introduce the suffixes *-ly, -ful, -ness,* and *-able.* Write *friend.* Beneath it write *friendly.* What do you call a word part added at the end of a base word? (suffix) Run your hand beneath *friendly.* Have students identify *friend* as the base word and *-ly* as the suffix. Explain that the suffix

-ly means "characteristic of." When you do something in a friendly way, you do it in a way that is characteristic of how a friend does it. Have students read the two parts together: *friend, ly, friendly.*

Use the same process to guide students in reading the words below. Explain the meaning of each suffix: *-ful* means "full of," *-ness* means "state of," and *-able* means "can be done." Discuss the meaning of each word.

exactly	wonderful	quickness	avoidable

If… students cannot read a word,
then… use Routine Card 4 to help students identify its parts.

On Their Own For more practice, have students complete Worktext p. 70 and work together to read the Word List words.

Common Syllables and Multisyllabic Words

Objectives:
- Introduce common syllables *-tion, -sion, -ion.*
- Introduce common syllables *-ture, -tive.*
- Introduce multisyllabic words.

MATERIALS
- Worktext pp. 71–73
- Routine Cards 1, 4
- Letter tiles

Set the scene Remind students that many words are made of more than one syllable. Explain that in today's lesson they will learn to read multisyllabic words, some of which end with one of several common syllables.

Routine **1. Connect** Write *puzzle* and *struggle.* How many syllables do these words have? What do you notice about the final syllable? (It ends with consonant plus *le.*) This lesson focuses on words that end in the syllables *-tion, -sion,* and *-ion.*

2. Model and Give Examples Write and say *vacation.* Help students identify the three syllables: *va, ca, tion. Vacation* is one of many words that ends with *-tion.* Cover *vaca* and have students read *-tion* with you several times. Repeat the process to introduce the syllable *-sion* in *conclusion* and *-ion* in *opinion.*

3. Model Blending Write *inspection.* Notice the letters *-tion.* These letters often make up the last syllable of a word. When you see a word that ends in *-tion,* divide the word just before these letters. Then divide the first part of the word into syllables. Point to the syllables *in, spec,* and *tion.* Read the syllables one after the other to say the word with me: *in, spec, tion.* Repeat the process with *mansion* and *region.* Have students read the words and then identify the syllables in each word. Develop word meaning by asking questions (for example, *Have you ever performed an inspection? When, and why? What does a mansion look like? What region of the United States do you live in?*). Challenge pairs of students to use each word in a sentence.

Mini-Lesson 1 — Syllables *-tion, -sion, -ion*

Remind students that...
- Many words include common syllables.
- Many words end with the syllables *-tion, -sion, -ion.*

Word List

affection	division
corruption	champion
collision	

Guide Practice
Explain that in this lesson students will practice reading words that end with *-tion, -sion,* and *-ion.* Write and say *adoption.* When you see a word ending with *-tion,* remember to divide the word just before these letters. Read the three syllables one after the other to say the word: *a, dop, tion, adoption.* Then write *vision* and *champion* and help students identify their *-sion* and *-ion* endings.

Repeat the procedure to have students read the words below. Encourage students to discuss the meaning of each word. Ask volunteers to take turns using each word in a sentence.

location	position	expansion
tension	billion	onion

If... students cannot read a word,
then... help them identify one syllable at a time as you cover the remaining syllables. Model sound-by-sound blending, reading each individual syllable before reading the whole word (Routine Cards 1, 4).

On Their Own For more practice, have students complete Worktext p. 71 and guide them in reading and spelling the words on the Word List.

Mini-Lesson 2 — Syllables -*ture*, -*tive*

Remind students that...
- Many words include common syllables.
- Many words end with the syllables –*ture*, -*tive*.

Word List

adventure	competitive
creature	festive
signature	negative

Guide Practice

Use steps 2 and 3 of the routine to guide students in reading words that end with the common syllables -*ture* and -*tive*. Write and say *culture*. *Culture* has two syllables. Cover -*ture* and read the first syllable: *cul*. Then cover *cul* and read the second syllable: -*ture*. When you see a word that ends with -*ture*, divide the word just before these letters. Read the syllables one after the other to say the word. Have students read with you: *cul, ture, culture*.

Repeat the procedure with the words below. Discuss the meaning of each word. Have students work in pairs to make up a sentence that uses each word.

culture	future	structure
attractive	active	creative

If... students cannot read a word,

then... model blending the sounds in each syllable and then ask students to blend them with you.

On Their Own Use Worktext p. 72 and the Word List for additional practice. Help students build the Word List words with letter tiles and break each into syllables.

Mini-Lesson 3 — Multisyllabic Words

Remind students that...
- Many words include common syllable patterns.
- Recognize syllable patterns in multisyllabic words to make them easier to read.

Word List

cleanliness	disconnecting
fictional	relocation
remarkable	unrecognizable

Guide Practice

Help students read and divide many multisyllabic words. Remember, when you read a long word, look for meaningful parts. Write this sentence: *The food looked unappealing.* Point to *unappealing* and discuss its meaning. Ask what smaller word parts students see at the beginning and end of this word. (prefix *un*, *appeal*, and ending -*ing*) What do these parts mean? (not, to be pleasing or attractive, continuous action) To read the word, I say each chunk slowly and then say them quickly: *un, appeal, ing, unappealing*.

Guide students in reading the words below. Work together to break the words into meaningful parts or chunks. Use each word in a sentence and invite students to discuss the words' meanings.

misbehaving	decoration
unacceptable	unselfishness

If... students cannot read a word,

then... model reading the word parts as you run your hand beneath them (Routine Card 4).

On Their Own For additional practice, have students complete Worktext p. 73 and practice reading and spelling the Word List words.

Objectives:

- Teach concept of inflectional endings.
- Introduce endings *-ed, -ing* that require doubling the final consonant.
- Introduce endings *-er, -est.*
- Introduce endings *-ed, -ing* with **silent *e*** words.

MATERIALS

- Worktext pp. 74–76
- Routine Cards 2, 4
- Letter tiles

Set the scene Remind students that they have learned to read base words that have endings *-ed* and *-ing* added to them. In this lesson, we will learn about words that require spelling changes when you add these and other endings.

Routine **1. Connect** Write *count, counted,* and *counting.* Invite volunteers to read each word and use it in a sentence. Remind students that the *-ed* ending of a verb shows past tense, or past time. (Give sample sentences, such as *Today you count. Yesterday you counted.*) When you add *-ed* and *-ing* to some words, their spellings change before the ending is added.

2. Model and Give Examples Write and say *grab, grabbed,* and *grabbing.* What is the vowel sound in *grab?* (short *a, /a/*) Whenever I see a short vowel word that ends in just one consonant (point to *b*), I know I have to double the consonant before I add the endings *-ed* and *-ing.* Circle the two *b*'s in *grabbed* and *grabbing.* Repeat the process with *stop, stopped,* and *stopping.*

3. Model Blending Run your hand under *grab.* Have students blend it with you: /g//r//a//b/. When you see a word with *-ed* at the end, break the word into smaller parts. Point to *grabbed.* The parts are *grab* and *-bed.* Read the parts one after the other with me: *grab, bed, grabbed.* Repeat the process with *grabbing* and word part *-ing.* Ask pairs of students to use each word in a sentence. Then say *shop, shopped,* and *shopping.* Challenge volunteers to identify the word parts in *shopped* and *shopping* and spell each word.

Mini-Lesson 1 Endings *-ed, -ing*: Double Final Consonant

Remind students that…

- Many words can be broken up into smaller word parts.
- In many words the final consonant is doubled before the endings *-ed* and *-ing.*

Word List

chopped	chopping
grinned	grinning
scanned	scanning
shrugged	shrugging

Guide Practice

Use the routine to help students read words that double the final consonant when you add endings *-ed* and *-ing.* Write and say *beg.* What do you notice about the vowel sound in this word? (It makes the short *e, /e/* sound.) When you see a short vowel word that ends with just one consonant (point to *g*), you need to double that consonant

before you add endings *-ed* or *-ing.* Write *begged* and *begging.* Read the word parts with me to say each word: *beg, ged, begged; beg, ging, begging.*

Provide additional practice with the words below. Discuss the meaning of each word with students.

blurred/blurring	chatted/chatting
dropped/dropping	solved/solving

If… students cannot read a word,
then… use Routine Cards 2 and 4 to help them identify each word part and blend the whole word.

On Their Own For additional practice, use Worktext p. 74 and the Word List. Help children use letter tiles to spell and read each word on the list.

Mini-Lesson 2 — Endings *-er, -est*

Remind students that...
- Many words can be broken into smaller word parts.
- Many words end with the word parts *-er* and *-est.*

Word List
bigger	biggest
softer	softest
dimmer	dimmest
wetter	wettest

Guide Practice
Help students learn to spell and read words with endings *-er* and *-est.* Write and say *small.* Add *-er.* We use the ending *-er* when we compare two things. What are the two parts of this word? (*small* and *-er*) Let's read the parts together: *small, er, smaller.*

Repeat with *-est* and *smallest.* Explain that *-est* is used to compare three or more things. Read the word with me: *small, est, smallest.*

Then write *thin.* Beneath it, write and say *thinner* and *thinnest.* Point to the second *n.* Notice that with some words, you double the final consonant before you add *-er* or *-est.* When you see a short vowel word that ends with just one consonant (write *sad* and point to *d*), you need to double the consonant before adding *-er* or *-est.* Help students read the words below. Use each in a sentence.

calmer/calmest	flatter/flattest
lighter/lightest	slimmer/slimmer

If... students cannot read a word,

then... run your finger under each sound-spelling as you blend the base word. Then add *-er* or *-est* and say the whole word.

On Their Own For additional practice, use Worktext p. 75 and the words in the Word List.

Mini-Lesson 3 — Endings *-ed, -ing*: Drop Final *e*

Remind students that...
- Many words can be broken into smaller word parts.
- In many words, like *skate* and *drive,* the final *e* is silent.
- When you add *-ed* and *-ing* endings to words that end with **silent *e*,** drop the *e.*

Word List
dozed	dozing
guided	guiding
shaded	shading
lived	living

Guide Practice
Remind students that they have learned to add *-ed* and *-ing* endings to many words. Today you'll learn to add *-ed* and *-ing* to words that end with **silent *e*.** Write *blame.* *Blame* has a silent *e.* Blend the sounds: /b//l//ā//m/. When a word ends with a silent *e,* drop the *e* before you add *-ed.* Erase the *e* and add *-ed.* Ask students to say the base word, *blame,* and then the ending one after the other: *blame, ed, blamed.* Follow the procedure to guide students in spelling and reading *blaming.*

Give students more practice with the words below. Ask students to use each word in a sentence.

hoped/hoping	pasted/pasting
piled/piling	shined/shining

If... students cannot read the words,

then... have them identify one part at a time as you cover the remaining parts (Routine Card 4).

On Their Own Have students complete Worktext p. 76. For additional practice, guide them in reading and spelling the words on the Word List. Encourage discussion of each word's meaning.

Plurals

Objectives:
- Teach the concept of plurals.
- Review plural words that end in -s or -es.
- Review plural words that end in -ves.

MATERIALS
- Worktext pp. 77–79
- Routine Cards 2, 4, 10
- Letter tiles

Set the scene Write *snack* and *lunch.* These words are singular. Today we'll learn how to make plural words that mean "more than one," such as *snacks* and *lunches.* Remind students that they can break many words into smaller parts. We'll learn about changing word parts to form plural words.

Routine **1. Connect** Write *subject* and *classmate.* Have students read the words aloud. We are going to make plural words by adding *-s* to these words.

2. Model and Give Examples Point to *subject.* Have a volunteer name a subject people learn about in school. We can add the ending *-s* to *subject* to make a new word that means "more than one subject" Add *-s.* Cover the *-s* and read the base word aloud: *subject.* Then cover the base word and read the ending *-s*: /s/. Uncover the entire word. *Subjects* is a plural word that means "more than one subject." Repeat the process to form the plural of *classmate.*

3. Model Blending Tell students that when they see a word with *-s* at the end, they should notice the word part *-s* and the base word. Point to *subjects.* In this word, the base word is *subject,* and the word part is *-s.* Read them one after the other: *subject, -s, subjects.* Point to the base word and word part *-s* in *classmates.* Read them to say the word: *classmate, -s, classmates.*

Mini-Lesson 1 Plural *-s*

Remind students that...
- Many words consist of smaller word parts.
- Plural words refer to more than one person, place, thing, or idea.
- Many plural words end in *-s.*

Word List
guards	basketballs
crosswalks	swimmers
teammates	opponents
games	

Guide Practice
Tell students they will learn to use the ending *-s* to mean "more than one." Write *hallway.* Run your hand under the syllables and say the word: *hall way.* Add *-s.* When you see a word with *-s* at the end, try reading the parts one after the other. Run your hand under *hallway* and then the ending *-s.* Have students say *hallway, -s, hallways.*

Hallways is a plural word that means "more than one hallway." Ask a volunteer to explain where one might find hallways.

Repeat the procedure with the words below. Explain that the ending *-s* can stand for the sound /s/ or the sound /z/.

teachers	parents	problems	answers

If... students cannot read a word,
then... break the word into parts and have students repeat them. Use Routine Card 10 to help students understand and practice reading the word.

On Their Own See Worktext p. 77 and the Word List for additional practice. Help students build plural words with letter tiles.

Mini-Lesson 2 — Plural -es

Remind students that...
- Many words are made up of smaller word parts.
- Plural words refer to more than one person, place, thing, or idea.
- Many plural words end in **-es.**

Word List

bosses	bunches
sunglasses	axes
latches	mixes

Guide Practice

Remind students that they make some plural words by adding *-s.* Today we'll learn the plural forms of words that end with *s, ch,* and *x.* To make words that end with those letters mean "more than one," we add **-es.** Write and say *bench.* Circle the *ch.* This word ends in *ch.* We can add *-es* to the end of *bench* to make a plural word. Write *benches.* Point to the ending *-es.* The base word is *bench,* and the word part is *-es.* Let's read them one after the other: *bench, -es, benches.* **Have a volunteer use *benches* in a sentence.**

Repeat the procedure to guide practice with the words below.

classes	passes	pitches
punches	boxes	reflexes

If... students cannot read a word,

then... use Routine Cards 2 and 4 to model blending sounds in the base word and identifying word parts.

On Their Own For additional practice, use Worktext p. 78. Have students use letter tiles to form words from the Word List.

Mini-Lesson 3 — Plural *f* or *fe* to *v*

Remind students that...
- They can break many words into smaller word parts.
- Plural words refer to more than one person, place, thing, or idea.
- Some plural words end in **-ves.**

Word List

scarves/scarf	lives/life
leaves/leaf	dwarves/dwarf
halves/half	

Guide Practice

Remind students that they have added *-s* or *-es* to form plural words. Today we'll form plural words by changing some letters at the end of singular words. Write *bookshelves.* Circle the letters *ves.* Plurals that end in *ves* are often made from singular words that end in *f* or *fe.* If I take away the word part *-es* and change the *v* to *f* or *fe,* I can figure out the singular word. **Model that process and** write *bookshelf.* Point to the word. You know *bookshelf. Bookshelves* is a plural word that means more than one *bookshelf.* Ask students to explain what bookshelves are.

Follow the same procedure to guide practice with these word pairs.

hooves/hoof	loaves/loaf
yourselves/yourself	wolves/wolf

If... students cannot read the words,

then... run your hand under each part as you say the word together.

On Their Own For additional practice, use Worktext p. 79 and the Word List. Ask students to use letter tiles to change each plural to its singular form.

Phonics and Decoding Lesson 27
Compound Words

Objectives:
- Teach the concept of compound words.
- Review a strategy for reading compound words.

MATERIALS
- Worktext pp. 80–82
- Routine Cards 2, 4
- Letter tiles

Set the scene Remind students that they have learned how to combine word parts into new words. You've practiced making new words by adding a word part to a word you know. Today you will learn to read **compound words,** or words made of two or more shorter words.

Routine **1. Connect** Write *class* and *room.* You know these words. Let's read them: *class, room.* What is a class? (Pause for responses.) What is a room? (Pause for responses.) Today we'll learn how to make a new word, called a compound word, by putting these words together.

2. Model and Give Examples Point to *class* and *room.* We can add *room* to the end of *class* to make a new word. Write *room* at the end of *class* to make *classroom.* Cover *room* and read *class.* Then cover *class* and read *room.* Finally, read the new word: *classroom. What is a classroom?* (Pause for responses.)

3. Model Blending Point to the word parts *class* and *room.* In this word the parts are *class* and *room.* Have students read the word with you: *class, room, classroom.* Then write *doormat.* Help students identify the word parts in *doormat.* Have them read the word with you: *door, mat, doormat.* Remind students that to read a compound word, they should break the words into parts and say the shorter words one after the other.

Mini-Lesson 1 — Compounds

Remind students that...
- Many words consist of smaller word parts.
- A compound word is made from two or more shorter words.

Word List
rainbow	artwork
hillside	sunroom
housefly	downtown

Guide Practice
Use step 3 of the routine above to help students read **compound words.** Write *haircut* and have students identify the words that form *haircut.* Run your hand under *hair.* The first short word is *hair.* Run your hand under *cut.* The second short word is *cut.* To read a compound word, read the two words one after the other: *hair, cut, haircut.* Ask a volunteer to use *haircut* in a sentence. Repeat the procedure to guide practice with the words below.

sidewalk	doghouse	highchair
runway	bookcase	

If... students struggle to read a compound word, **then...** help them identify one part at a time as you cover the other part (Routine Card 4).

On Their Own For more practice, use Worktext p. 80 and the Word List. Have students use letter tiles to form each word part and read each compound word.

Mini-Lesson 2 — More Compounds

Remind students that...
- Many words consist of smaller word parts.
- A compound word contains two or more shorter words.
- Many compound words build on a common base word.

Word List

houseplant	daylight
schoolhouse	lighthouse
workbench	songbird
homework	birdcage

Guide Practice

Remind students how to make a compound word. Write *suit.* We can add *case* to the end of *suit* to make a new word. Write *case* after *suit.* Point to *suit* and then to *case.* Let's read the word parts together: *suit, case, suitcase.* Write *suit* again. Many compound words share a base word. Write *swim* before *suit* and point to each word. Let's read the word parts together: *swim, suit, swimsuit.*

Ask a volunteer to use *suitcase* and *swimsuit* together in a sentence.

Repeat the process with the words below. Help students think of other words that share the base words *ball, over,* and *up.*

meatball	ballroom	takeover
overpower	makeup	upstairs

If... students cannot read a word,
then... use Routine Card 2 to practice blending the whole word from its parts.

On Their Own See Worktext p. 81 and the Word List for additional practice. Ask students to take turns using each word in a sentence. Help students with sound-by-sound blending as needed.

Mini-Lesson 3 — Compounds with a Longer Word Part

Remind students that...
- Small word parts can be combined in a longer word.
- A compound word is made of two or more shorter words.
- Some compound words have a longer word as a word part.

Word List

afterthought	businesslike
everyone	underground
steelworker	timekeeper
popcorn	

Guide Practice

Remind students how to put two words together to make a compound word, such as *haircut.* Explain that some compound words contain a longer word as one part. Write *hair* and *brushes.* You know these words. We can make a compound word by putting a short word, *hair,*

together with a longer word, *brushes.* Cover *brushes* and read the first word: *hair.* Then cover *hair* and read *brushes: brushes.* Read the word with me: *hair, brushes, hairbrushes.* When do people use hairbrushes? (Pause for responses.)

Repeat the procedure to guide practice with the words below.

potholder	prizewinner	uppermost
eyeglasses	schoolteacher	

If... students cannot read the words,
then... help them say the two smaller words and then read them with you without pausing.

On Their Own For additional practice, use Worktext p. 82 and the Word List.

Phonics and Decoding Lesson 28
More Endings and Plurals

Objectives:
- Review ending *-es* to words that end in **y**.
- Review ending *-ed* to words that end in **y**.
- Review irregular **plurals**.

MATERIALS
- Worktext pp. 83–85
- Routine Cards 1, 2, 4
- Letter tiles

Set the scene Remind students that they already know how to make plural words. You also know how to read words that end in **y**. Today we'll learn how to add the endings *-es* and *-ed* to words that end with y. Later we'll learn more ways to make **plurals**.

Routine **1. Connect** Write *bury* and *study*. Point to *bury*. You know this word. To bury a treasure, what would a person have to do? (Pause for responses.) Today we will learn how to change this word and others like it into new words by adding the ending *-es*.

2. Model and Give Examples Point to *bury*. When we see a word ending in y, we change the y to an *i* before we add an ending. The *i* keeps the sound of the y in the word. Erase the y and replace it with *i*. Then add *-es*. Cover the *-es* and say *bury*. Remember, I changed the y to an *i*. Uncover the *-es,* point to it, and say the new word: *buries*.

3. Model Blending Point to the *-es*. When I see a word with *-es* at the end, I figure out the base word. A y might have been changed to an *i*. Point to the *i*. I read the two parts: *buri, -es, buries*. Have a volunteer use *buries* in a sentence. Repeat the procedure with *study*.

Mini-Lesson 1 — Ending *-es*: Spelling Change **y** to *i*

Remind students that...
- Word parts can be added to many words.
- Adding an ending sometimes requires a spelling change.
- Before adding *-es* to a word that ends in **y,** change the **y** to an *i*.

Word List
vary/varies
deny/denies
fry/fries
enemy/enemies
family/families

Guide Practice
Write *party* and beneath it write *parties*. We can put the word parts *party* and *-es* together to make the word *parties*. What does *parties* mean? Pause for responses; accept both noun and verb meanings. Invite volunteers to use *parties* in a sentence.

Point to *i* in *parties*. We change the y in *party* to an *i* before we add *-es*. Run your hand under *parties*. The parts of this word are *parti* and *-es*. Read them with me: *parti, -es, parties*.

Repeat the procedure with the word pairs below.
puppy/puppies   hurry/hurries   spy/spies
apply/applies   diary/diaries

If... students have difficulty reading a word,
then... remind them that the *i* in the new word keeps the sound of the y in the base word. Have students say both words, and return to the example later in the practice.

On Their Own Use Worktext p. 83 and the Word List for additional practice. Have students use letter tiles to form and read each word part.

Mini-Lesson 2 — Ending -ed: Spelling Change y to i

Remind students that...
- New words can be formed by adding word parts to a base word.
- For some words, adding an ending requires a spelling change.
- Before adding **-ed** to a word that ends in **y,** the **y** must be changed to an **i.**

Word List

worry/worried	envy/envied
carry/carried	supply/supplied
marry/married	

Guide Practice

Write *worry* and beneath it write *worried.* Before we add anything to the end of *worry,* we have to change the *y* at the end (point to *worry*) to an *i.* Point to *worried* and then cover the *-ed.* Before we add **-ed** to a word ending in *y,* we change the *y* to an *i.*

Point to *worried* again. Let's say the base word and the ending together, one after the other, to say the word: *worri, -ed, worried.* The *i* keeps the same sound as the *y.* Ask a volunteer to explain what *worried* means.

Repeat the procedure to guide practice with the word pairs below.

copy/copied	pry/pried	reply/replied
try/tried	cry/cried	

If... students cannot read a word,
then... have them identify one part at a time as you cover the other part or parts (Routine Card 4). Use Routine Card 1 to practice sound-by-sound blending.

On Their Own See Worktext p. 84 and the Word List for additional practice.

Mini-Lesson 3 — Irregular Plurals

Remind students that...
- A plural word names more than one person, place, thing, or idea.
- For many words, the plural is formed by adding an ending.
- Irregular plural words are different from their singular forms.

Word List

goose/geese	man/men
ox/oxen	child/children

Guide Practice

Remind students that they know plural words that end in *-s* and *-es,* such as *goats* and *foxes.* You also know words like *wolf* that have a spelling change to make the plural *wolves.* The spelling of irregular **plurals** does not follow any pattern. You must learn and remember these words.

Write *tooth.* Ask students for the word that means "more than one tooth." *Teeth* is the plural of *tooth.* Write *teeth.* Point to *oo* in *tooth* and *ee* in *teeth.* The vowels in these words are different. For other irregular words, such as *sheep,* the singular and plural words are exactly the same.

Repeat the procedure to help students read and define the word pairs below.

foot/feet	woman/women
mouse/mice	person/people

If... students cannot read a word,
then... use Routine Card 2 to blend the separate sound-spellings. Have students repeat the sounds after you without pausing.

On Their Own For more practice, use Worktext p. 85. For additional practice, help students read the words on the Word List.

Phonics and Decoding Lesson 29
Contractions

Objectives:

- Review the concept of contractions.
- Review contractions *n't, 'm.*
- Review contractions *'s, 'd.*
- Review contractions *'re, 've, 'll.*

MATERIALS

- Worktext pp. 86–88
- Routine Card 4

Set the scene Remind students that they know the words *not, am, is, has, had, would, are, have,* and *will.* Today we'll use these words to make **contractions.** A contraction is a short word made by combining two words and leaving out some letters. We use an apostrophe to replace the letters we leave out.

Routine **1. Connect** Write *not* and *am.* Today we'll learn how to make new words by putting *not* or *am* together with another word.

2. Model and Give Examples Write *couldn't. Couldn't* is a contraction for the words *could not.* Write *could not.* A contraction is a short way of writing two words as one word. We write the words together and take out one or more letters. Point to the apostrophe. This is an apostrophe. It takes the place of the letter *o* in *not.* Erase the *o* in *not* and insert an apostrophe in its place. Circle *n't* in *couldn't.*

3. Model Blending Point to *couldn't.* When I see a word with an apostrophe, I know it might be a contraction. I notice the two parts. In this word, the parts are *could* and *n't.* I say the parts together to read the word: *could, n't, couldn't.* Have students repeat the word with you, and invite a volunteer to use *couldn't* in a sentence.

Mini-Lesson 1   Contractions *n't, 'm*

Remind students that…

- Word parts can be added to many words to make new words.
- A contraction is a shorter word formed by combining two words.
- In a contraction, an apostrophe replaces omitted letters.
- Some contractions include *n't,* and only one word contains *'m.*

Word List

wasn't	hadn't
shouldn't	isn't
doesn't	I'm

Guide Practice

Help students connect *n't* with *not* and *'m* with *am.* Write *are not* and *aren't.* Point to *aren't.* We can put the words *are* and *not* together to make the contraction *aren't.* Point to the apostrophe. The apostrophe takes the place of the

letter *o* in the contraction *aren't.* The two parts in *aren't* are *are* and *n't.* Have students read the two parts and the word with you: *are, n't, aren't.* Ask a volunteer to use *aren't* in a sentence.

Repeat the procedure to introduce the word pairs below.

have not/haven't	**did not/didn't**
would not/wouldn't	**I am/I'm**

If… students have difficulty reading a contraction, **then…** use Routine Card 4 to help them identify one word part at a time. Run your hand under the word as they read each part.

On Their Own Use Worktext p. 86 and the Word List. Have students identify the two words that formed each contraction and use each contraction in a sentence.

Mini-Lesson 2 Contractions 's, 'd

Remind students that...

- Adding word parts can make new words.
- A contraction is formed by combining two words.
- In a contraction, the omitted letters are replaced with an apostrophe.
- Many words include the contractions 's or 'd.

Word List

she is/she's   we would/we'd

what has/what's   you had/you'd

he had/he'd

Guide Practice

Write *it's, it is, she'd,* and *she had. It's* is a contraction. You know that a contraction is a short way of writing two words. The apostrophe takes the place of letters that have been left out. Erase the *i* in *is* and insert an apostrophe in its place. Point to *it's.* Let's read the parts in the contraction together to say the word: *it, 's, it's.* Ask a volunteer to use *it's* in a sentence.

Repeat the procedure with *she'd* and *she had.* Explain that, depending on the sentence, *'s* can also stand for the word *has,* and *'d* can also stand for *would.*

that is/that's   he has/he's

they had/they'd   I would/I'd

If... students cannot read a contraction,

then... identify the word parts and have students read the parts one after the other with you.

On Their Own See Worktext p. 87 and the Word List for additional practice. Have students use each contraction in a sentence.

Mini-Lesson 3 Contractions 're, 've, 'll

Remind students that...

- Word parts can be combined to make new words.
- A contraction is a shorter word formed by combining two words.
- In a contraction, an apostrophe replaces the omitted letters.
- Many words include the contractions 're, 've, or 'll.

Word List

they're   we'll

I've   I'll

they've   they'll

you've

Guide Practice

Remind students that contractions always contain apostrophes. Today we'll read contractions in which *'re* replaces *are, 've* replaces *have,* and *'ll* replaces *will.*

Write *we are* and *we're.* Combining *we* and *are* makes the contraction *we're.* Point to the apostrophe. This apostrophe takes the place of letters that are left out. Erase the *a* in *are* and insert an apostrophe in its place. Circle *'re* in *we're.* Put the parts together to read the word: *we, 're, we're.* Who can use *we're* in a sentence? (Pause for responses.) Point out that *'re* can also stand for *were.*

Repeat the procedure to introduce the contractions below.

you are/you're   we have/we've   you will/you'll

If... students cannot read a word,

then... read the word parts together as you run your hand beneath them.

On Their Own For more practice, use Worktext p. 88. Using the Word List, have students identify the two words that formed each contraction.

Possessives and Abbreviations

Objectives:

- Review concepts of *possessives* and *abbreviations.*
- Review rule for forming possessive of singular words.
- Review rule for forming possessive of plural words.
- Review common abbreviations.

MATERIALS

- Worktext pp. 89–91
- Routine Cards 1, 2, 4

Set the scene Remind students that they can add endings to make new words. You've learned to read contractions that contain apostrophes. In this lesson, we'll learn to make new words by adding endings with apostrophes and periods.

Routine

1. Connect Write *hasn't. Hasn't* is a contraction made of the words *has* and *not.* The apostrophe replaces the *o* in *not.* Today we'll make new words that contain apostrophes.

2. Model and Give Examples Write *teacher's desk.* Point to *teacher's. Teacher's* is a **possessive** word. A possessive word shows that a person, group, or animal owns or has something. Read both words. Circle the *'s* ending. Whose desk is it? The teacher owns, or has, the desk. Repeat the process with *Brian's homework.*

3. Model Blending Point to the apostrophe and *s* in *teacher's.* If I take away the apostrophe and the *s,* the word *teacher* is left. The apostrophe and *s* tell me that the desk belongs to one teacher. Add an apostrophe and *s* to a singular word to make it possessive.

If you see a word with an apostrophe and *s* at the end, the word might be possessive. To be sure, you have to read the whole sentence. Repeat steps 2 and 3 with the name of a student in the group.

Mini-Lesson 1 Singular Possessives

Remind students that...

- A singular word names one person, place, thing, or idea.
- A possessive shows that a person, group, or animal owns or has something.
- Adding letters or parts to a word can make new words.
- To make a singular word possessive, add an **apostrophe** and *s.*

Word List

sister's	crowd's
father's	hummingbird's
orchestra's	violinist's

Guide Practice

Write *coat. Coat* is a singular word. It names one thing. Beneath *coat,* write *coat's. Coat's* is a possessive word. Write *buttons* after *coat's* and read the phrase: *coat's buttons.* The **apostrophe** and *s* tell me that the buttons belong to the coat. Circle the apostrophe and *s.* The

apostrophe comes before the *s.* To make a singular word possessive, add an apostrophe and *s.*

Repeat the process with the possessives below. Explain that the *s* sometimes stands for the sound /s/ and other times the sound /z/.

family's	grandmother's	neighbor's
hamster's	butterfly's	

If... students have difficulty reading a word, **then...** ask for the sound of each letter or group of letter, and then use Routine Card 2 to help students blend the words.

On Their Own Use Worktext p. 89 and the Word List for additional practice. Help students write each singular word and its possessive. Ask them to use the possessive in a sentence.

Mini-Lesson 2 — Plural Possessives

Remind students that...
- A plural word names more than one person, place, thing, or idea.
- A possessive shows that a person, group, or animal owns or has something.
- To make a plural word that ends in *s* possessive, add an **apostrophe.**
- To make a plural word that does not end in *s* possessive, add an **apostrophe** and *s.*

Word List

ladybugs'	kids'
hotels'	children's
wolves'	mice's

Guide Practice

Write *shark* and *the shark's teeth*. Point to *shark* and then to *shark's*. *Shark* is a singular word, and *shark's* is a singular possessive. Now write *sharks* and *the sharks'*

teeth. Point to *sharks* and then *sharks'*. *Sharks* is a plural word, and *sharks'* is a plural possessive. Circle the **apostrophe.** The apostrophe comes after the *s,* so I know that the teeth belong to more than one shark. If a plural word ends in *s,* add an apostrophe to make it possessive.

Write *men. Men* is also a plural word. For this kind of plural, add an apostrophe and *s* to make the possessive: *men's.*

Repeat the procedure with the words below.

teammates'	parents'	dwarves'
families'	people's	

If... students cannot read a word,
then... point out the *'s* ending (Routine Card 4) and model sound-by-sound blending (Routine Card 1).

On Their Own See Worktext p. 90 and the Word List for additional practice. Help students use each possessive word in a sentence.

Mini-Lesson 3 — Abbreviations

Remind students that...
- An abbreviation is a shortened form of a word.
- Many common abbreviations begin with a capital letter and end with a period.

Word List

Feb./February	D.C./District of Columbia
Nov./November	Capt./Captain
Fri./Friday	Rte./Route

Guide Practice

Write *Mr. Montoya* and say it aloud. Point to *Mr.* This abbreviation is a shortened form of the word *Mister.* An abbreviation begins with the same capital letter as the whole word. An abbreviation ends with a period.

Write *Mister.* All letters in an abbreviation come from the whole word. Circle the *M* and *r* in *Mister.* We learn abbreviations by thinking about the whole word and

remembering the shortened form. When we read an abbreviation out loud, we usually say the whole word.

Write the following abbreviations and words. Point to each abbreviation and have students read the word it represents.

Ave./Avenue	Dr./Doctor
Wed./Wednesday	Oct./October
U.S./United States	

If... students cannot decode an abbreviation,
then... circle the letters the abbreviation shares with the word, and say the word with students.

On Their Own Use Worktext p. 91 for additional practice. For more practice, write abbreviations from the Word List. Help students identify the whole word each abbreviation represents.

Phonics and Decoding
Student Worktext

Name _____

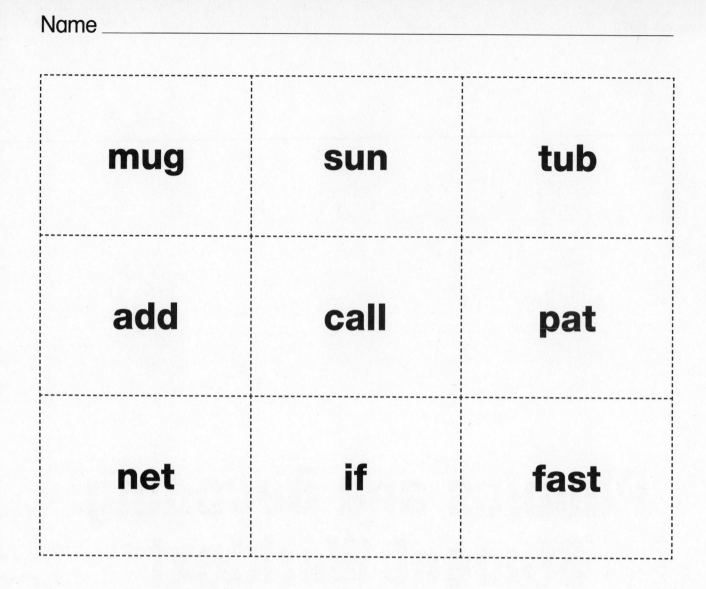

mug	sun	tub
add	call	pat
net	if	fast

Pat is a fan.
Sam is fit.
Sam runs for fun.

Directions Have your child cut out the word cards. Place the cards face down. Then have your child pick a card and identify the first letter of the word and read the word. Help your child use the word in a sentence. Then read the sentences at the bottom together with your child.

Phonics and Decoding Lesson 1

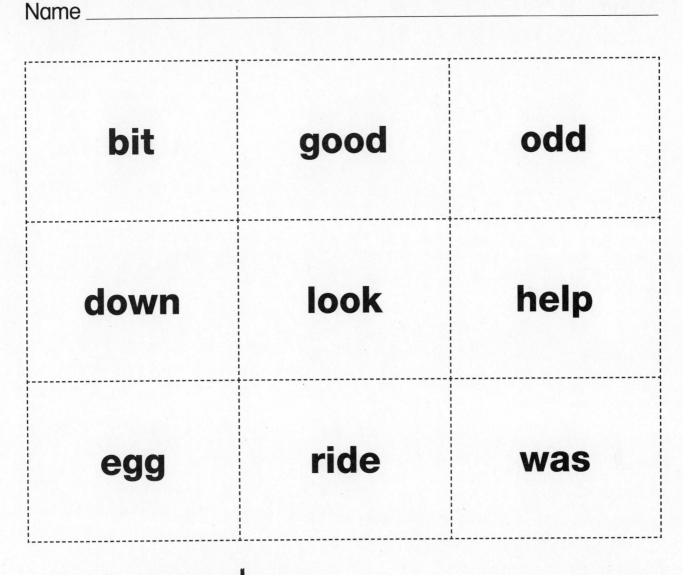

bit	good	odd
down	look	help
egg	ride	was

Bob put the top on the pot.
Did Tom drop an egg?
Tom got the mop.

 School + Home

Directions Have your child cut apart the word cards. Place the cards in a bowl. Take turns with your child picking a card and reading the word. Then have your child identify the first letter of each word and use the word in a sentence. Then read the sentences at the bottom with your child.

jump	**kid**	**under**
vet	**yes**	**zip**
quick	**box**	**jet**

Max is a pup in a tub.
Rub-a-dub-dub, Pup.
Max is quick. He zips.

 School +Home

Directions Have your child cut apart the word cards. Choose a word and ask your child to identify the first letter of the word. Then have your child read the word and use it in a sentence. Finally, help your child read the sentences at the bottom.

Name _____

bring	**class**	**trap**
crow	**grin**	**black**
flip	**plug**	**front**
grill	**gloss**	**sled**

The frog is sleeping in the grass by the tree.
My plan is to grab it from the back.

Directions Point to each word and have your child read it. Then have him or her cut apart the word cards. Have your child sort the words into two piles: words that begin with *l* blends and words that begin with *r* blends. Take turns choosing a card and using the word in a sentence. Finally, have your child read the sentences aloud.

School + Home

Phonics and Decoding Lesson 2   Initial Blends and Three-Letter Blends   **5**

Name _____

1. We want to _____ in the pool.
(sit, swim)

2. How do you _____ that word?
(spell, say)

3. Dad ate a _____ before he left.
(sandwich, snack)

4. The coach said to _____ running.
(start, practice)

5. Maria drew a _____.
(seal, snowflake)

6. Why did Sam _____ at the clock?
(glance, stare)

We used a stick to stir the small fire.
We sang and told scary stories.
Stan stayed snug in the sleeping bag.

Directions Have your child read the first sentence and the two words in parentheses underneath. Ask your child which word has an *s* blend (*swim, spell, snack, start, snowflake, stare*). Have him or her circle the correct word and write it in the blank. Repeat with each sentence. Then have your child read the sentences at the bottom to you and circle the nine words that begin with an initial *s* blend.

Phonics and Decoding Lesson 2

Word Bank

snack	sing	squeeze	splat	scoop	slip
scrape	spread	soft	stare	strong	spring

1. _____   _____

2. _____   _____

3. _____   _____

4. _____   _____

5. _____   _____

6. _____   _____

Sue screamed when she saw the squirrel.
Did it squeak back?

Directions Ask your child to read the words in the Word Bank. Then have your child find the six words that have three-letter blends (*squeeze, spring, strong, splat, scrape, spread*) and write them on the lines. In the second column, help your child write other words with these three-letter blends. Finally, have your child read aloud the sentences at the bottom.

School + Home

Name ________________________________

Word Bank

plant	spend	blind
stamp	left	raft

1. Did your rubber __________ float?

2. That red __________ is a flower.

3. We can __________ twenty dollars.

4. That letter needs a __________.

5. I __________ my winter coat at school.

6. The __________ man had a large dog.

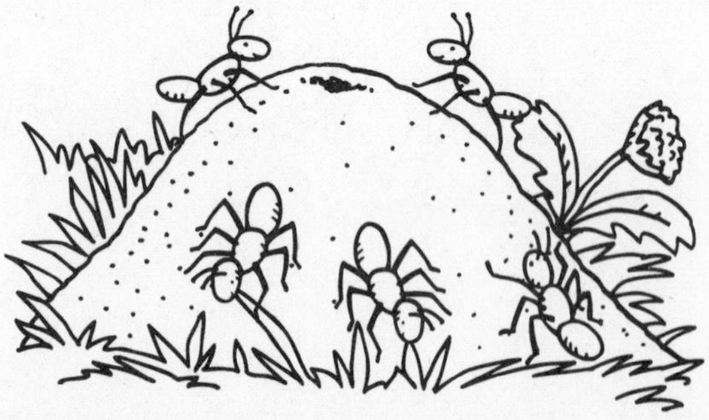

The grass is damp and soft.
Do you see the ant by your left hand?

School + Home

Directions Ask your child to read each word in the Word Bank and circle the final blend in each word. Then have your child read each sentence and write the word from the Word Bank that completes each sentence. Then have your child read each sentence and the sentences at the bottom aloud.

Name _____

1. gulp	scalp	puppy	help
2. bolt	spent	built	quilt
3. child	told	shield	wilt
4. scold	shelf	wolf	elf
5. field	sold	halt	wild
6. colt	insult	knelt	golf
7. gold	build	ground	mild

Sam felt bad.
He needs help with his belt.
He told us it broke.

Directions Today your child learned about words that end with *lt, ld, lp,* and *lf* blends. Tell your child that three of the four words in each row end with the same two letters. One does not. Ask your child to identify and circle the word with the different final blend. Help your child use each word in a sentence. Finally, have your child read the sentences at the bottom to you.

Name _____

| sk | sp | st |

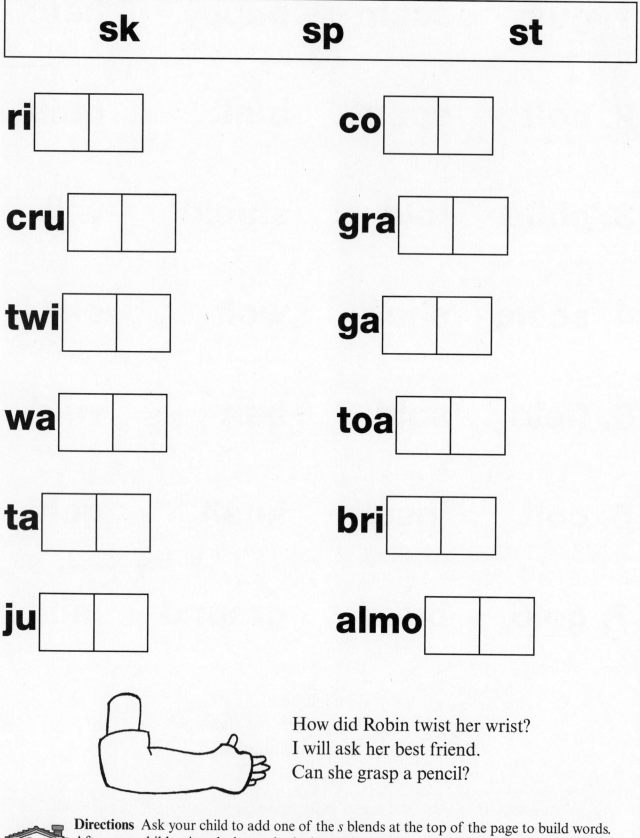

ri ☐☐

co ☐☐

cru ☐☐

gra ☐☐

twi ☐☐

ga ☐☐

wa ☐☐

toa ☐☐

ta ☐☐

bri ☐☐

ju ☐☐

almo ☐☐

How did Robin twist her wrist?
I will ask her best friend.
Can she grasp a pencil?

School + Home

Directions Ask your child to add one of the *s* blends at the top of the page to build words. After your child writes the letters in the boxes, have him or her read the word aloud. Work together to use each word in a sentence. Finally, have your child read the sentences at the bottom to you.

Phonics and Decoding Lesson 3

fish   flash   squish

shop   shower   shove

trash   brush   crash

share   shock   flash

mash   fresh   sharp

She saw a small shark near the ship.
Should she throw it a fresh fish?

Directions Your child learned to read words with *sh*. Have your child read each word aloud. Tell your child to draw a circle around words that begin with *sh* and underline words that end with *sh*. Take turns using each word in a sentence. Finally, have your child read aloud the sentences at the bottom.

Name _____

1. Tell your friend the _____.

2. Our house is _____ of the city.

3. _____ you for the gift.

4. I _____ the movie is great.

5. My brother has a loose _____.

6. The rain made the _____ damp.

I will go to camp for three days next month.
Thirty other girls will be there with me.

Directions Have your child read each word in the Word Bank and circle the *th* digraph. Then have your child read each numbered sentence. Ask him or her to find the word in the Word Bank to finish each sentence and write it on the line. Finally, have your child read the sentences at the bottom to you.

Name _____

Word Bank		
phone	photo	rough
laugh	cough	graph

1. what a camera takes _____

2. not smooth _____

3. like a giggle _____

4. sign of a cold _____

5. use to make calls _____

6. kind of chart _____

Ralph is my nephew.
His soccer team won a big trophy.
He took a photo of it.

Directions Have your child read the words in the Word Bank and circle the digraphs (*ph* or *gh*) that stand for /f/. Then read the first numbered item aloud. Tell your child to find the word in the Word Bank that matches that description. Ask your child to write the word on the line. Continue until your child has matched all the words. Finally, read the sentences at the bottom together.

School + Home

Name _____

Word Bank

heart	hatch	stop	chess	card	chimney
stretch	cold	bunch	clue	home	chose

---

1. She picked a _____ of flowers.

2. Pat likes to play _____.

3. You should _____ before you run.

4. Did the egg _____ yet?

5. I _____ a sandwich for lunch.

6. Smoke went up the _____.

Did the tree branch scratch the child's cheek?
No, but it did touch her hair.

Directions Ask your child to read each word in the Word Bank and circle the words with the /ch/ sound as in *check*. Then have your child read each numbered sentence. Ask him or her to use one of the circled words to finish each sentence. Have your child write the word on the line. Then have your child read each sentence and the sentences at the bottom aloud.

where	**white**	**whistle**
whale	**wheat**	**what**
wheel	**why**	**which**
whip	**when**	**whisper**
whiff	**while**	**whether**

What do you want—white or wheat bread?
When will lunch be ready?
Where should I sit, and which plate is mine?

School + Home

Directions Choose a word, say it aloud, and ask your child to circle the word you said. Have your child make up a sentence that uses the word. Continue until your child has circled all the words. Finally, have your child read the sentences at the bottom to you.

Name _____

| chord | chef | ache |
| chute | machine | echo |

ch spells /k/	ch spells /sh/

The pots were made of chrome.
The chef dropped one down a chute.
The noise echoed through the house.

Directions Have your child cut apart the word cards. Ask your child to circle the letters *ch* in each word. Tell your child to place the word in the left column if *ch* stands for /k/ (as in *chord*). If *ch* stands for /sh/ (as in *brochure*), have your child place the word in the right column. Finally, help your child read the sentences. Have your child point to each word that includes the letters *ch*.

Name _____

Word Bank

clock   sock   trucks
     stick   quack

Across

1.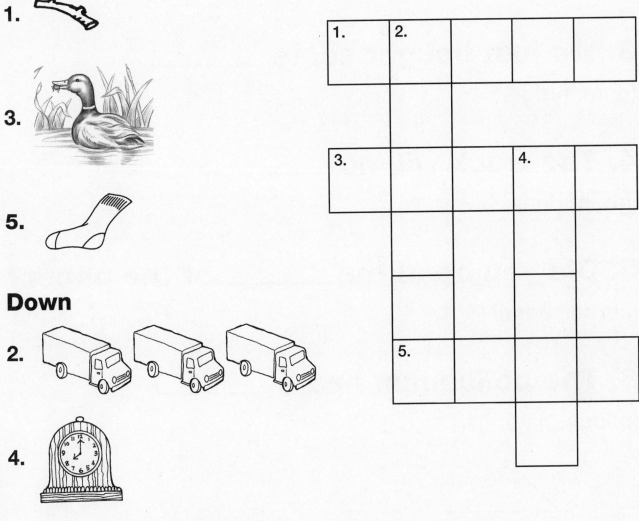

3.

5.

Down

2.

4.

Jack will pack his black bag.
Did he check the lock?

School + Home

Directions Have your child look at each picture and decide which word in the Word Bank matches it. Have your child write the word in the correct spot in the puzzle. Continue until the puzzle is complete. Then have your child read the sentences aloud.

Name _____

1. The _____ crosses the Red River.

(guy, bridge)

2. Is your father a _____?

(judge, grandfather)

3. We just bought some _____.

(gum, fudge)

4. The truck will not _____.

(go, budge)

5. Did you bend the _____ of the paper?

(corner, edge)

6. The policeman had a _____.

(badge, bag)

See that smudge on the edge of the picture frame.
Do you have any knowledge of what caused it?

Directions Have your child read the first sentence and the two words in parentheses below. Ask your child which word would make sense to fill in the blank. Have him or her circle the correct word. Repeat with each sentence. Then have your child read the sentences at the bottom to you. Tell your child to circle the words that end with *dge*.

18 Final Digraphs and Sounds

phonics and Decoding Lesson 6

Name _____

bring	wrong	hang	rung	king
blank	skunk	honk	wink	rank

The pink pig drank a lot of water.
We should bring him more from the sink.

Directions Have your child read the words at the top aloud and then cut apart the word cards. Ask your child to sort them by final sounds. Give the *nk* word cards to your child and keep the *ng* word cards yourself. Play tic-tac-toe. Substitute *ng* words for X's and *nk* words for O's. Have your child read each word aloud before it is placed on the grid. After you have played several games, have your child read the sentences to you.

School + Home

Name _____

1. The ___ is on the sand.   ◯ grab   ◯ jab   ◯ crab

2. I ate a big ___ of
pancakes.   ◯ lack   ◯ stack   ◯ tack

3. We ___ in the cold lake.   ◯ swam   ◯ slam   ◯ ram

4. Please ___ the present
today.   ◯ wrap   ◯ clap   ◯ slap

5. That box is thin and ___.   ◯ brat   ◯ flat   ◯ mat

6. Write your name in the ___.   ◯ tank   ◯ rank   ◯ blank

The fat cat drank the milk.
Dad saw a black patch on its back.

Directions Have your child read the set of words in each item and circle the letter pattern the three words share (-ab, -ack, -am, -ap, -at, -ank). Then read each sentence. Tell your child to fill in the bubble in front of the word that will complete each sentence. Take turns using the other two words in sentences. Finally, ask your child to read the sentences at the bottom aloud.

School +Home

Name _____

Word Bank

mop	kick	chick	knob	ring	swing
shot	clip	chill	flop	knot	drill

1. _____

2. _____

3. _____

4. _____

5. _____

6. _____

Will Dad use a drill to fix the grill?
After that job, can he fix the door knob?

Directions Read each word in the Word Bank. Then point to the first word and ask your child if it matches one of the pictures. If it does, have your child write the word on the line to the left of the picture. If a word does not match a picture, move to the next word. Repeat until your child has written a word to match each picture. Finally, ask your child to read the sentences aloud.

Name _____

-unk	-ug	-ed	-eck

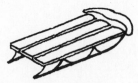

Fred gave a red sled to Ted.
Fred found it in a trunk with some junk.

Directions With your child, take turns explaining each word's meaning and using it in a sentence. Then read the four word parts aloud. Point to -*unk*. Tell your child to find all the words in the Work Bank that end in -*unk* and write them on the lines in the first column. Continue the process with the other endings until your child has sorted and written all the words. Finally, have your child read aloud the sentences.

School + Home

1. class	cement	calm	city
2. center	crazy	circus	clock
3. slice	pick	cider	coat
4. cool	trace	chill	pencil
5. place	crazy	sick	citizen
6. cough	calm	celery	cell
7. nice	city	climb	music
8. claim	once	cake	price

The circus is a great place!
That clown had a nice smile on his face.

Directions Today your child learned to read words with the soft *c* sound as in *mice* and *city*. Each numbered row includes two words with the soft *c* sound. Have your child read aloud the words in each row and then circle the two soft *c* words. Work together to make up a sentence that uses the two soft *c* words in each row. Finally, have your child read the sentences at the bottom to you.

Name _____

1. Did you clean the bird cage? _____

2. That big dog is gentle. _____

3. Glen sang a song on stage. _____

4. Did you go to the gym? _____

5. A germ made me get sick. _____

6. I gave Gus a giant box. _____

7. We heard a huge bang. _____

Our car engine makes a strange noise.
I hope it is not a huge problem.

Directions Today your child learned to read words with the soft *g* sound as in *gem* and *logic*. Each sentence contains one word with a soft *g* sound. Have your child read each sentence and circle the soft *g* word in the sentence. Then have your child write the word on the line. Finally, have your child read aloud the sentences at the bottom.

School + Home

24 More Consonant Sounds

Phonics and Decoding Lesson 8

Name _____

Word Bank				
wise	supper	send	his	best
pants	dogs	these	last	yells

1. _____ _____

2. _____ _____

3. _____ _____

4. _____ _____

5. _____ _____

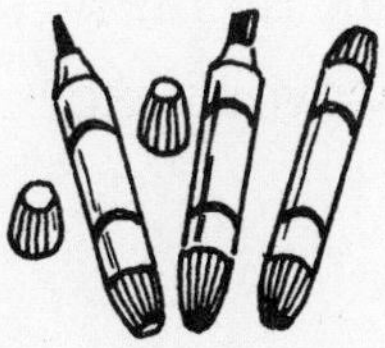

He chose to draw those frogs.
He will use these pens and markers.

Directions Ask your child to read the words in the Word Bank and circle the five words that have /z/ spelled *s* as in *toys*. Then have your child write the words on the lines. In the second column, help him or her write other words with /z/ spelled *s*. Then take turns using each word in a sentence. Finally, read the sentences at the bottom together.

School + Home

Name _____

1. The ___ took off on time. ◯ car ◯ plane ◯ bus

2. Did Jake ___ the pie? ◯ make ◯ buy ◯ eat

3. The ___ was rocky and cold. ◯ park ◯ cave ◯ path

4. Did you get lost in the ___? ◯ city ◯ maze ◯ mall

5. Ana is ___. ◯ tall ◯ brave ◯ smart

6. Did James ___ to you? ◯ talk ◯ wave ◯ speak

Jane came to the zoo with me.
A male lion shook its mane at us.
Then it made a strange face.

School + Home **Directions** Read aloud each sentence and the words to the right. Tell your child to fill in the bubble for the word that has the long *a* sound spelled *a_e* as in *wake*. Finally, ask your child to read aloud the sentences at the bottom.

Word Bank

slime	pipe	glide	spice	slide	bite
smile	time	kite	prize	knife	fire

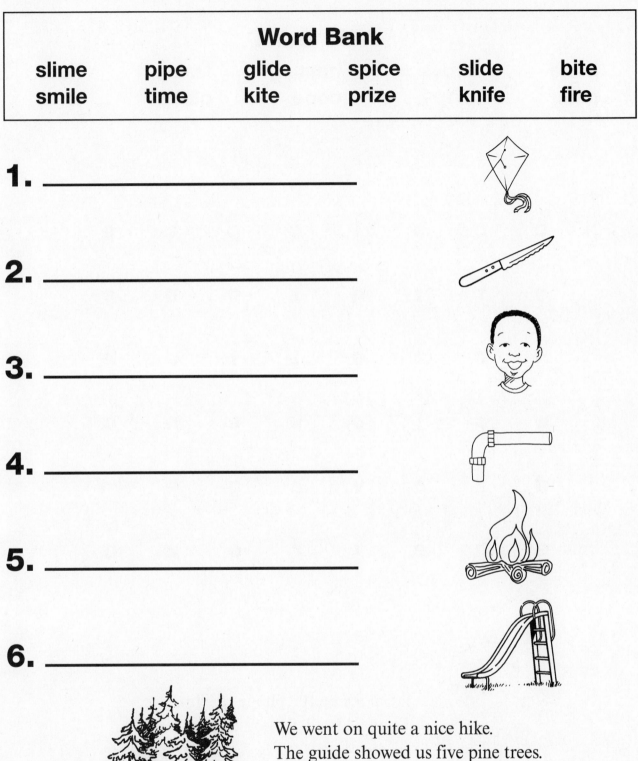

1. _____

2. _____

3. _____

4. _____

5. _____

6. _____

We went on quite a nice hike.
The guide showed us five pine trees.

Directions Point to the first word in the Word Bank. Have your child read it. Ask your child if it matches one of the pictures. If it does, have your child write the word on the line next to the picture. If a word does not match a picture, move to the next word. Repeat until your child has read all the words and written a word to match each picture. Finally, ask your child to read the sentences aloud.

School + Home

Name _____

Word Bank

bone	drove	home	froze	note
pole	slope	cone	globe	joke

```
c  o  s  l  o  p  e  p
o  r  l  g  l  o  b  e
n  o  t  e  j  l  o  h
e  s  j  o  k  e  n  o
d  r  o  v  e  g  e  m
e  h  e  f  r  o  z  e
```

Al spoke on the phone to Tim.
I hope Al will get home soon.

Directions Have your child read each word in the Word Bank. Take turns using each word in a sentence and explaining its meaning. Then ask your child to find each Word Bank word in the puzzle and circle it. Tell your child to look for words that go across and down. Finally, have your child read the sentences aloud.

scene	these	huge	mule	eve
fume	theme	cube	scheme	use

The photo was from last June.
The scene is cute.
The tree looks huge.

Directions Have your child cut apart the word cards. Ask your child to read the words and sort them into two piles: one for words with the long *u* sound (like *mule*) and one for words with the long *e* sound (like *Steve*). Keep one pile and have your child take the other. Then play tic-tac-toe. Substitute long *u* words for X's and long *e* words for O's. After you have played several games, have your child read the sentences to you.

School + Home

Name _____

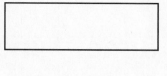

1. Remove the **s.**

2. Change the **e** to **i.**

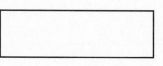

3. Change the **h** to **s**
and add **gn.**

4. Change the **s** to **m** and
replace the **gn** with **nd.**

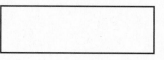

5. Change the **i** to **o** and
replace the **nd** with **st.**

6. Replace the **m** with **h.**

She and he said hi to Rick and me.
No, we did not go to the lake with them.

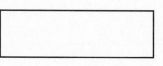
Directions Have your child follow each direction to make a new word. Explain that each new word comes from the word before it. Have him or her write the words on the lines. Take turns making up sentences that use two of the words together. Finally, have your child read the sentences at the bottom to you.

Phonics and Decoding Lesson 10

Name _____

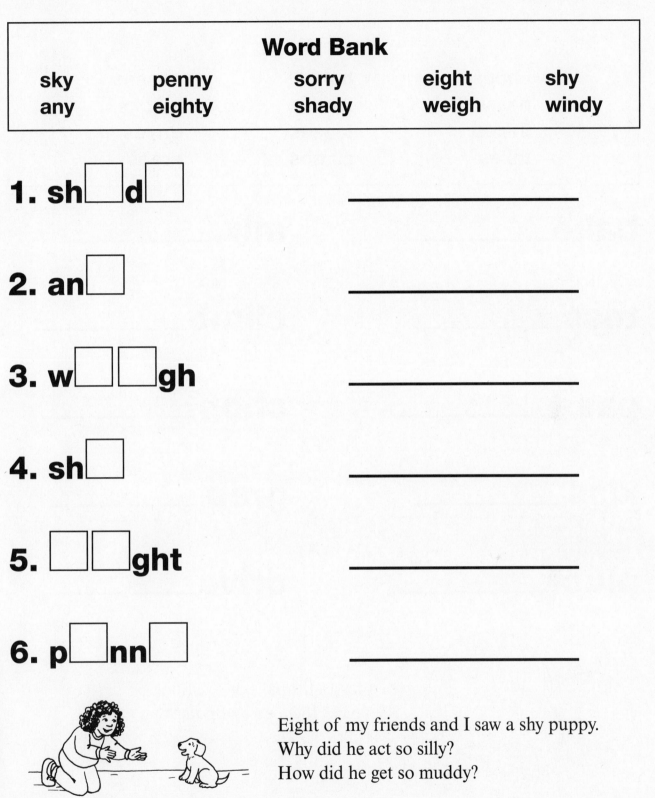

Word Bank

sky	penny	sorry	eight	shy
any	eighty	shady	weigh	windy

1. sh☐d☐ _____

2. an☐ _____

3. w☐☐gh _____

4. sh☐ _____

5. ☐☐ght _____

6. p☐nn☐ _____

Eight of my friends and I saw a shy puppy.
Why did he act so silly?
How did he get so muddy?

Directions For each item, have your child decide what letters are needed to build one of the words in the Word Bank. (Explain that not all words in the Word Bank will be used.) Have your child write the letter(s) in the boxes and then write the whole word on the line. Take turns using each word in a sentence. Finally, have your child read aloud the sentences at the bottom.

School + Home

Name _____

bake_____   mix_____

toss_____   climb_____

pass_____   chop_____

kiss_____   grab_____

pluck_____   drive_____

Ken tosses the balls on the floor.
Kim picks them up and puts them in
neat piles.

Directions Read the Word Bank. Help your child write the letter *s* or the letters *es* at the end
of each word to match a word in the Word Bank. Ask your child to read aloud each new
word and use it in a sentence. Then ask him or her to read the sentences at the bottom aloud
and circle each word that ends in -*s* or -*es*.

Name _____

Word Bank					
blasted	walked	ticked	tacked	planted	chanted
started	harmed	clicked	checked	mended	tricked

1. The rocket _____ off.

2. We _____ the poster to the wall.

3. Have you _____ the seeds yet?

4. The strong winds _____ the tree.

5. I _____ how to spell the word.

6. My mom _____ the hole in my shirt.

We walked to the pond and watched
the ducks.
Then we returned home and rested.

Directions With your child, take turns reading the Word Bank aloud. Then read each sentence aloud. Ask your child to decide which word in the Word Bank completes the sentence. Have him or her write the word and read the completed sentence aloud. Then have your child read the sentences at the bottom to you and underline each word that ends with -ed.

School + Home

building	**spying**	**crunching**
going	**dusting**	**rocking**
pulling	**showing**	**camping**
blushing	**melting**	**smashing**
singing	**puffing**	**crossing**

Beth likes reading, doing math, and going shopping.
Seth likes cooking, watching movies, and playing chess.

Directions Choose a word, say it aloud, and ask your child to point to the word you said. Then have your child think of and say a sentence that uses the word. Have your child circle the word. Continue until your child has circled all the words. Finally, have your child read the sentences at the bottom aloud and circle each word that ends in the word part -*ing*.

1. wel|come   Monday   until

2. market   napkin   picnic

3. hopping   rabbit   sudden

4. convince   frantic   escape

5. helmet   always   thirteen

6. basket   happen   yellow

We always make a shopping list.
We may not go shopping until Thursday.

School + Home

Directions Ask your child to read the three words in each row aloud. Have him or her draw a line between the syllables. (See the first word as an example.) Work together to make up a sentence that uses at least two of the words. Then have your child read the sentences at the bottom aloud.

Name _____

lo	nus	sic	do
ro	zor	tel	ra
mu	nate	stu	ven
bo	e	ger	lip
tu	ho	ren	si
cal	dent	bot	ti

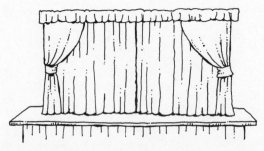

The music will start in a moment.
Please sit beside me.

Directions Have your child read the words in the Word Bank and draw a line between the syllables. Then have your child cut apart the syllable cards and build each word in the Word Bank by placing two syllable cards together. Ask your child to read each word aloud and use it in a sentence. Finally, have your child read the sentences at the bottom.

School + Home

Phonics and Decoding Lesson 12

Name _____

ard	ume	ic	ise
el	ic	ish	ace

pan_____   van_____

pal_____   vol_____

liz_____   prom_____

shov_____   com_____

Did you finish reading the novel?
No, I just began the second chapter.

Directions Have your child cut apart the syllable cards and lay them face down. Then have him or her select one at a time and place it next to a letter combination to build a word. Have your child say the word and use it in a sentence. Finally, ask your child to read the sentences at the bottom aloud.

Word Bank

harp	scarf	arm	cart
farm	shark	jar	park

Across

2. a big fish

4. item of clothing

7. where kids play

8. body part

Down

1. a container

3. makes music

5. carries things

6. might have a barn

Did you start your garden last March?
Was it hard to dig up the yard?

School + Home

Directions Help your child use the clues to complete the crossword puzzle. Have your child write the correct word from the Word Bank for each blank. Continue until the puzzle is complete. Then ask your child to read the sentences aloud.

Phonics and Decoding Lesson 13

Name _____

or	ore	oar

n_____th   r_____

m_____   bef_____

f_____ce   st_____m

sh_____   c_____n

_____der   t_____

ch_____   w_____n

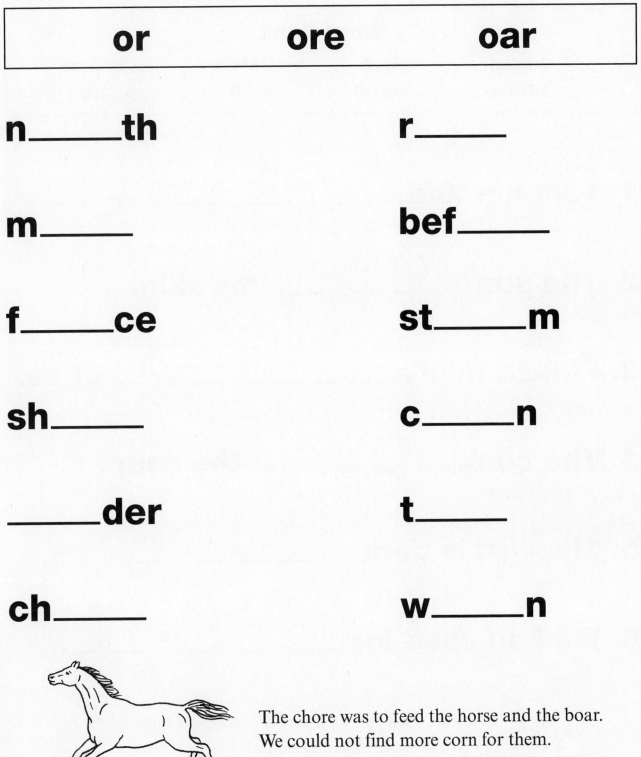

The chore was to feed the horse and the boar.
We could not find more corn for them.

Directions Help your child add *or*, *ore*, or *oar* to build words. After your child writes the letters on the line, have him or her read the word aloud and use it in a sentence. Finally, have your child read the sentences at the bottom and circle each word that contains the letters *or*, *ore*, or *oar*.

Phonics and Decoding Lesson 13   *R*-Controlled Vowels **39**

Name ____________________

Word Bank

purple	stern	thirsty	dessert
stirs	burns	curb	picture

1. I am hot and _ _ _ _ _ _ _.

2. The sun _ _ _ _ _ my skin.

3. Please take a _ _ _ _ _ _ _ of us.

4. The cook _ _ _ _ _ the soup.

5. My shirt is dark _ _ _ _ _ _.

6. We had cake for _ _ _ _ _ _ _.

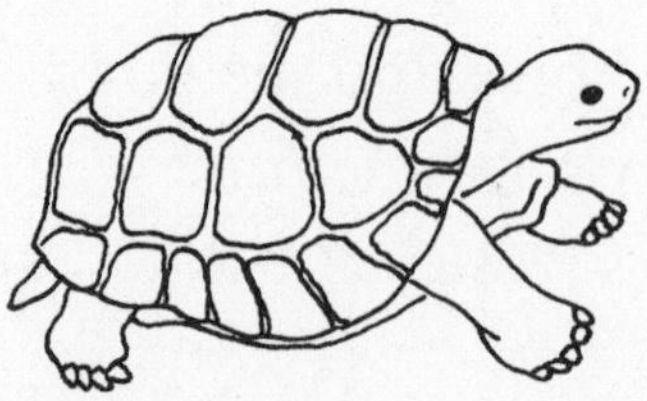

Riddle: I am a slow mover, but I am never far from home.
What am I?

School + Home **Directions** Have your child read the words in the Word Bank and circle the *r*-controlled vowels (*ur, er, ir*). With your child, find a word in the Word Bank to finish each sentence. Then have your child read the riddle and then read the letters in the circles (from top to bottom) to answer it.

Name _____

1. agree   name   sheep   better

2. learn   trace   either   keep

3. kneel   ape   they   sleep

4. camel   cheese   steel   echo

5. queen   chore   blue   ceiling

6. packed   peels   bent   glee

7. nice   seize   keen   myself

8. speech   seven   cake   receive

I need some ice for my knee.
Either a bee or a wasp stung it when I was sleeping.

Directions Today your child learned to read words with the long *e* sound (spelled *ee*, as in *green*, and *ei*, as in *neither*). Have your child read the words in each row aloud and then circle the two words that include the long *e* sound. Take turns using each of the words in a sentence. Finally, have your child read the sentences at the bottom to you.

Phonics and Decoding Lesson 14   Vowel Digraphs (Long *e* and *a*)   **41**

Name _____

1. Ken cleaned the garage. _____

2. Did the team win the game? _____

3. My bead necklace broke. _____

4. Each test has five questions. _____

5. When did you leave the house? _____

6. They drank tea and ate cake. _____

7. I felt weak after the race. _____

My dog gets lean meat at his main meal.
I sneak some really good treats to him too.

Directions Today your child learned to read words with the long *e* sound (spelled *ea*), as in *beach*. Have your child read each sentence and circle the word that has the long *e* sound. Then have your child write the word on the line. Finally, have your child read the sentences at the bottom and circle each word with a long *e* sound.

Phonics and Decoding Lesson 14

Name _____

Word Bank

cart	decay	praise	waist	raisin	apple	essay
trains	flat	mark	walk	claims	ask	spray

1. Will wrote his _____ on Japan.

2. The runner _____ every day.

3. A _____ is a dried grape.

4. Dr. Lee spoke about tooth _____.

5. Please _____ water on the plants.

6. The pants fit around my _____.

We went away for the holiday today.
The train was delayed.
We waited in the rain.

Directions Ask your child to read the words in the Word Bank and circle words with the long *a* sound as in *day*. Have your child read each sentence and use one of the circled words to complete it. Have your child write the word on the line. Then have your child read the sentences at the bottom and circle the words with *ai* and *ay*.

School + Home

Name _____

1. The _____ was painted _____.

| yellow | window |

2. Her _____ were sore from mixing the _____.

| dough | elbows |

3. Matt made me so mad I could have _____ a _____ at him.

| thrown | pillow |

4. The girls acted bravely, _____ they did not _____ what might be hiding behind the _____.

| know | boulder | although |

Kim left the mower in the driveway.
Jack stowed the shoulder bag below the seat.

 Directions With your child, read each sentence and fill each blank. Read the completed sentence aloud together. Then have your child read the sentences by the illustration and circle each word with the letters *ow* or *ou*.

44 Vowel Digraphs (Long *o* and *i*)

Phonics and Decoding Lesson 15

Name _____

Word Bank

presoak	haloes	railroad	petticoat
roadmap	tiptoe	woeful	backhoe

1. t ☐ ☐ t ☐ ☐

2. r ☐ ☐ ☐ m ☐ ☐

3. p ☐ ☐ ☐ i ☐ ☐ ☐ ☐

4. r ☐ ☐ ☐ r ☐ ☐ ☐

5. w ☐ ☐ f ☐ ☐

6. b ☐ ☐ k ☐ ☐ ☐

Noises echoed through the oak woods.
He sipped cocoa by the toasty coal fire.

Directions Read the words in the Word Bank together. Have your child complete each item by referring to the Word Bank. Say each completed word together. Then have your child read aloud the sentences at the bottom and underline each long *o* that is spelled *oa* or *oe*.

School + Home

Name _____

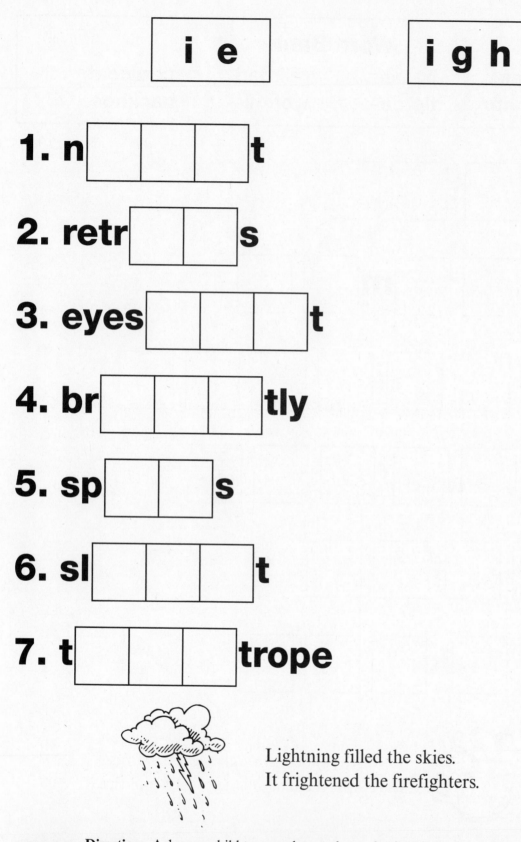

| i e | i g h |

1. n [ ][ ][ ] t

2. retr [ ][ ] s

3. eyes [ ][ ][ ] t

4. br [ ][ ][ ] tly

5. sp [ ][ ] s

6. sl [ ][ ][ ] t

7. t [ ][ ][ ] trope

Lightning filled the skies.
It frightened the firefighters.

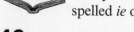

Directions Ask your child to complete each word using the letters at the top of the page. Then say the word in a sentence and invite your child to use it in a new sentence. Finally, have your child read the sentences and point to the words that contain the long *i* sound spelled *ie* or *igh*.

Word Bank

jealous	already	meadow
treasure	spread	ahead

1. **Al and Gina found the _____ure.**

2. **They found it _____d of the others.**

3. **Word _____d quickly.**

4. **Others were _____dy _____ous.**

5. **So Gina buried the treasure in a _____ow.**

Ocean weather is so pleasant.
I did not need my sweater at breakfast.

Directions For each blank, ask your child to find the correct word in the list above. Have your child write the missing part of the word on the line. When all sentences are complete, read the paragraph aloud. Then read the sentences at the bottom and have your child point to each word with the letters *ea*.

Name _____

1. We _____ in line for the movie.

2. You _____ like this song.

3. I gave her a _____ to read.

4. I _____ at the stove.

5. The wet dog _____ his coat.

6. Alex _____ at his watch.

You should hang your wool hood on a hook.
You could look at your book.

Directions With your child, read each word in the Word Bank and circle words with /ù/ such as *book*. Have your child complete the sentences using the circled words. Then ask your child to read the sentences at the bottom and point to each word with /ù/.

believe	**hockey**	**alley**
gooey	**chief**	**monkey**
key	**parsley**	**piece**
money	**thief**	**yield**

We took a brief journey.
We went through the valley on a trolley.

Directions Have your child cut apart the word cards and place them face down. Take turns picking up two cards. Say each word and then work together to make a sentence using both words. Continue the game until you have picked up all the cards. Finally, have your child read the sentences and circle each word with *ie* or *ey*.

School + Home

roo	goo	coo	hoo	too

1. Is your _____m big?

2. My dog likes to play and act _____fy.

3. Can I please have a s_____p of ice cream?

4. Where do you go to sc_____l?

5. The funny car_____n made me laugh.

The goose got loose in the school.
I found it roosting in the swimming pool.

Directions Silently read each sentence with your child. After each sentence, ask, "What do you think this sentence is about?" Then ask your child to use a group of letters from the box to fill in each blank. Say each completed sentence together. Finally, help your child read the sentences at the bottom fluently.

crewcut	soup	screwdriver	new
through	group	jewelry	grew

1. not old

2. many people

3. earrings, rings, watches

4. way to wear hair

5. something you eat

6. got bigger

She blew on her onion soup.
The huge crouton was hard to chew.

 **Directions** Read the words at the top aloud with your child. Have your child read each clue, or definition, aloud and then write the word that matches the definition in the box. Then read the sentences together and circle each word with /ü/ spelled *ew* or *ou*.

1. j ☐☐ cy   n ☐☐ sance

2. fr ☐☐ tful   purs ☐☐

3. cr ☐☐ se   swims ☐☐ t

4. gl ☐☐ d   cl ☐☐

5. bl ☐☐   br ☐☐ ise

6. overd ☐☐   untr ☐☐

The police recruit was in hot pursuit.
The cruiser blocked the avenue.

Directions With your child, complete each phrase by writing *ui* or *ue*. Have your child read each phrase aloud. Work together to make up a short sentence that uses each pair of words. Finally, have your child read aloud the sentences at the bottom and then repeat words that have *ui* or *ue* spelling the /ü/ sound.

ound

oud

cl   r   s   pr   f

p   h   l   m   al

The countess bounced to the ground.
The loud sound scared the count.

Directions Help your child combine beginning letters with the ending in each center oval to write words on the lines. Say each word with your child. Then read the sentences together, and have your child circle each word with *ou*.

Name _____

1. downtown	torn	crowd
2. toe	clown	powder
3. shower	show	towel
4. boat	flower	gown
5. hope	down	sow
6. how	chop	cow
7. crowd	roar	chow
8. however	book	now
9. downward	power	flow
10. vow	snow	tower

Wow! That sow has big teeth.
I wonder how the cow feels now.

School + Home

Directions Read the words aloud and have your child repeat them. Then help your child circle the two words in each row that have /ou/ spelled *ow*. Finally, read the sentences together, pointing to the words with /ou/ spelled *ow*.

Phonics and Decoding Lesson 18

Name _____

1. I hope you _____ **the trip.**

(enjoy, like)

2. Troy was _____ **by the bugs.**

(scared, annoyed)

3. Did you _____ **her for a game?**

(meet, join)

4. Please _____ **the eggs.**

(boil, eat)

5. Maria made the _____ **to go to China.**

(choice, decision)

The boys pointed at the royal convoy.
The queen enjoyed hearing their voices.

Directions Read each sentence with your child. Help your child choose the word in parentheses that has the /oi/ sound as in *toy* or *avoid*, and use it to complete the sentence. Ask your child to write the word on the line. Then read the completed sentence together. Conclude by having your child read aloud the sentences at the bottom.

Name _____

1. _____ me when you get home.

2. If you run down the hall, you may _____.

3. The beanstalk was _____.

4. We waltzed at the _____.

5. I buy _____ at the spice store.

The dog walker was tall.
He lifted the puppies off the asphalt.

Directions Help your child find the word from the Word Bank that completes each sentence. Have your child write the word on the line, read the sentence aloud, and then circle each /ȯ/ spelled *a* or *al*. Finally, read aloud the sentences at the bottom and emphasize each word with the /ȯ/ sound.

School + Home

Name _____

1. The cousins ran across the _____.

(lawn, haul)

2. Tran had his portrait _____.

(launched, drawn)

3. The sheriff caught the _____.

(outlaw, seesaw)

4. Finally, she _____ the train.

(paw, saw)

5. What _____ you to fall?

(drawl, caused)

6. Was the accident your _____?

(fault, authority)

Dawn scrawled her autograph.
She yawned and paused to straighten her shawl.

Directions Read each sentence aloud with your child. Have your child choose the word in parentheses that best completes the sentence, write the word on the line, and say the finished sentence. Read the sentences at the bottom together and ask your child to circle all the words on the page that have *au* and *aw*.

Name _____

naughty	**should**
sought	**showed how to do**
taught	**captured**
caught	**argued**
thoughtful	**likely to misbehave**
brought	**looked for**
fought	**kind and considerate**
ought	**carried with**

Lee coughed as he bought the popcorn.
He caught the cough from his daughter.

School + Home

Name _____

1. We learned to di<u>vide</u> and find per<u>cents</u>.

2. I com<u>plained</u> <u>a</u>bout the tear in my ma<u>roon</u> jacket.

3. The ma<u>rines</u> were sub<u>merged</u> in the la<u>goon</u>.

4. My aunt tells me to for<u>give</u>, for<u>get</u>, and act ma<u>ture</u> whenever I see that bully.

5. You need con<u>trol</u> to suc<u>ceed</u> on the tra<u>peze</u>.

Can you please adjust the dress for me?
It is about two inches too long.

School + Home

Directions Help your child read each sentence aloud. Explain that each word with an underlined syllable has a schwa sound in the *other* syllable. Have your child circle the letter that spells the schwa sound in each word. Then read aloud the sentences at the bottom.

Name _____

carrot	**kitchen**	**chicken**	**counter**
pepper	**measure**	**oven**	**sugar**
table	**toaster**	**pasta**	**timer**
cover	**blender**	**sprinkle**	**cupboard**
onion	**simmer**	**supper**	**breakfast**

_____

_____

_____

Father called us to dinner.
We like tuna salad with crackers.

Directions All of the words have the schwa sound in the second syllable. Have your child read the words aloud. Help him or her circle the vowel(s) that stand for the schwa sound in the second syllable. Work together to write one or more sentences using as many of the words as you can. Then read the sentences at the bottom and have your child repeat any words with the schwa sound.

School + Home

Phonics and Decoding Lesson 20

Name ______________________________

tkon ___ ___ ___ ___

elkne ___ ___ ___ ___ ___

ockkn ___ ___ ___ ___ ___

finke ___ ___ ___ ___ ___

unclekk

___ ___ ___ ___ ___ ___ ___

spacknak

___ ___ ___ ___ ___ ___ ___ ___

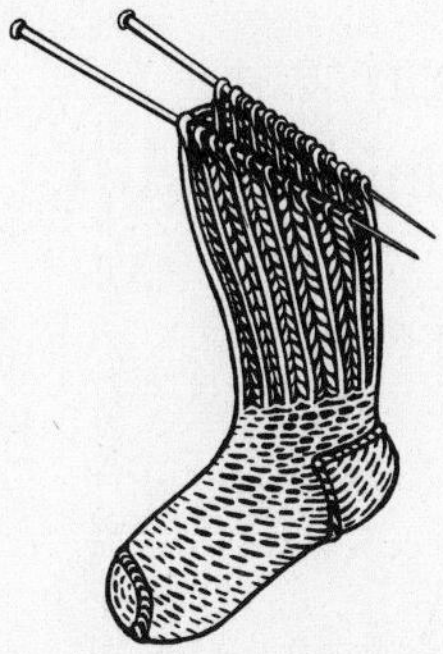

Nancy knew her knee socks were nice.
The nurse had a knack for knitting.

School + Home **Directions** Help your child unscramble, write, and pronounce each *kn* word (*knot, kneel, knock, knife, knuckle, knapsack*). Then read the sentences together and have your child circle each word with *kn* at the beginning.

Name _____

wrangle	**wrist**	**write**
wreck	**wrestle**	**wrap**
wrinkle	**wrench**	**wren**

Rick unwrapped the wrong present.
He rewrapped it with the wrinkled paper.

Directions Read the words aloud to your child, emphasizing /r/ spelled *wr*. Then have your child cut apart the word cards and place them face down. Take turns choosing a card, reading the word aloud, and using the word in a sentence. Finally, point to each silent *w* as you read the sentences at the bottom.

Phonics and Decoding Lesson 21

Name _____

1. **nimble**   **climber**   _____

2. **thumb**   **crumbling**   _____

3. **dumbbells**   **tomb**   _____

4. **numb**   **number**   _____

5. **nibbled**   **combed**   _____

6. **lamb**   **thimble**   _____

7. **bomb**   **tumbler**   _____

8. **stumble**   **dumb**   _____

The climber hid on a limb.
The bear munched on a honeycomb.

Directions Each row has a word with and without the silent *b* in *mb*. Help your child read each row aloud. When your child correctly pronounces a word with a silent *b*. Have your child correctly spell the words with the silent *b* on the line next to each word pair. Finally, read aloud the sentences at the bottom.

Name _____

Word Bank

bristles	campaign	hustle
gnawed	fasten	gnome

---

1. I must ~~hurry~~ _____, or I will miss the train.

2. There is a little ~~bearded man~~ _____ in the garden.

3. When she patted the hog, she felt its ~~pointy hairs~~ _____.

4. Many people helped her ~~run for election~~ _____.

5. You must ~~attach~~ _____ the straps to your parachute.

The horse gnawed on the thistle.
The cattle herder likes to whistle.

Directions Help your child read the words in the Word Bank and circle the silent letter in each word. Then help your child choose a word from the Word Bank to replace the crossed-out word or words in each sentence. Your child should write the new word on the line and then read the sentence aloud. When you finish the sixth sentence, read the sentences at the bottom together and circle each silent letter.

School + Home

Name _____

Word Bank

fable	vehicle	ankle	kettle
castle	puddle	uncle	angle

1. I sprained my _____.

2. The _____ had a happy ending.

3. Put the stew in the big _____.

4. The _____ needs new brakes.

5. A wall surrounds the _____.

6. My _____ is a plumber.

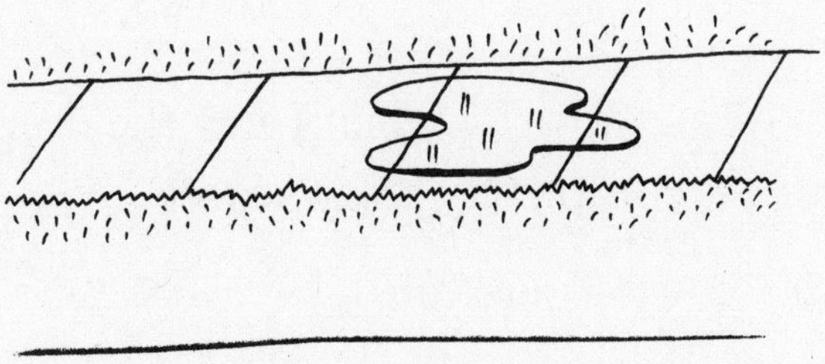

Meg dropped a single apple
into the puddle.
Her ankle got a little wet!

Directions Ask your child to find a word in the Word Bank to finish each sentence. Have your child write the word on the line and read each sentence. Finally, have your child read the sentences at the bottom and circle all the words on the page that end in *le*.

Word Bank

| improve | wrinkle | explode | embrace | dinner | contract |
| purchase | orchard | pebble | market | kingdom | surprise |

1. _____

2. _____

3. _____

4. _____

5. _____

6. _____

It was an extreme surprise when I saw the dolphin. In an instant, it completely disappeared.

Directions Have your child read the words in the Word Bank. Tell your child to circle the six words that have the VCCCV pattern (*improve, purchase, orchard, explode, embrace, kingdom, contract, surprise*). Have your child write those words on the lines and draw a line between the syllables. Take turns using each word in a sentence. Then have your child read aloud the sentences at the bottom.

1. riot	**sheep**	**robot**	**dial**
2. eight	**poet**	**built**	**cruel**
3. away	**meow**	**area**	**meal**
4. lion	**chaos**	**goose**	**spelling**
5. loud	**giant**	**react**	**fruits**
6. laugh	**Noah**	**diet**	**could**
7. create	**clue**	**rainy**	**fluid**

Leah played the violin,
and I listened to the radio.
Our area of the gym was
not quiet!

Directions Have your child find and circle the two words in each row that have two vowels together, each one spelling a different sound (such as *quiet* and *liar*). Ask your child to draw a line between the vowels to divide the circled words into syllables. Discuss the word meanings. Finally, have your child read the sentences aloud.

Phonics and Decoding Lesson 22   More Syllable Patterns **67**

renew _____

preschool _____

uncommon _____

unselfish _____

prepay _____

dishonest _____

Did you discover new topics to research?
Should we recopy our prewriting notes?
It's unclear when the paper is due.

Directions Ask your child to read each word and circle the prefix in each (*re-*, *pre-*, *un-*, or *dis-*). Tell your child to write a new word with a prefix on each line. Have your child read the new word and use it in a sentence. Finally, have your child read the sentences at the bottom and circle each word with a prefix.

School + Home

Name _____

Word Bank

logical	tailor	ageless	actor
preacher	seller	parental	

p a r e n t a l s

a c l g o e b o e

n t a i l o r g l

l o g i c a l o l

p r e a c h e r e

a g e l e s s e r

Did the visitor talk to the professional painter?
What makes the painting priceless?

Directions Have your child read each word in the Word Bank. Take turns using each word in a sentence and explaining its meaning. Then ask your child to find each word in the puzzle and circle it. Tell your child to look for words that go across and down. Finally, have your child read the sentences aloud.

Name ______________________________

1. Dan ________ eats lunch at noon.

(closely, usually)

2. She wore a ________ dress.

(fashionable, payable)

3. Who is the ________ of the orchestra?

(conductor, consumer)

4. She felt ________ in her leg.

(weakness, happiness)

5. The ________ girl danced well.

(graceful, armful)

6. I ________ stopped after two hours of running.

(costly, finally)

We eagerly bought that wonderful car.
It was affordable and had beautiful red seats.

School + Home **Directions** Have your child circle the word in parentheses that best completes each sentence. Then have your child read the sentences at the bottom aloud and circle all the words on the page that have the suffix *-ly, -ness, -ful,* or *-able*.

Word Bank

conclusion	vision	companion	position	accordion
division	opinion	champion	imitation	session

imita_____   **divi**_____

opin_____   **compan**_____

sess_____   **champ**_____

vi_____   **conclu**_____

posi_____   **accord**_____

In my opinion, the television fashion
show was boring.
It had little action, no emotion, and
silly clothes.

Directions Ask your child to read each word in the Word Bank and circle the final -*tion,*
-*sion,* or -*ion.* Then have him or her write the letters that are needed to complete each word.
Discuss the word meaning and help your child use each word in a sentence. Finally, have your
child read aloud the sentences at the bottom.

School + Home

Name _____

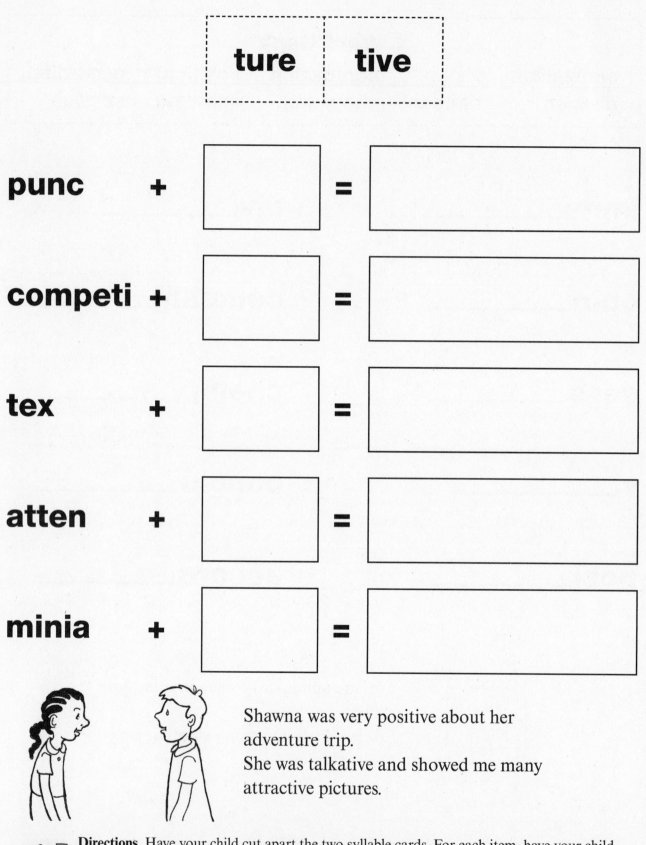

ture	tive

punc + [ ] = [ ]

competi + [ ] = [ ]

tex + [ ] = [ ]

atten + [ ] = [ ]

minia + [ ] = [ ]

Shawna was very positive about her adventure trip.
She was talkative and showed me many attractive pictures.

School + Home   **Directions** Have your child cut apart the two syllable cards. For each item, have your child place the correct card next to the first syllable to complete the word. Have your child read the word, use it in a sentence, and then write it in the bigger box. Finally, have your child read the sentences at the bottom to you.

Phonics and Decoding Lesson 24

Name _____

Word Bank

rebuilding   motionless   disrespectful

operation   principals

1. If you are _____, you don't move.

2. The doctor performed the _____.

3. Both school _____ are women.

4. _____ the sandcastle was hard.

5. Please do not be _____ to him.

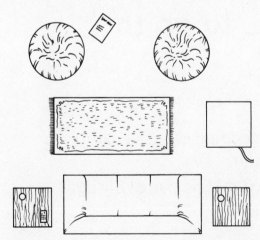

Will you reposition the new furniture?
The sofa is unexpectedly long.
I am disappointed.

Directions Help your child read each word in the Word Bank and circle the suffix or ending in each (*-ing, -less, -ful, -tion, -al*). Then help him or her read each sentence and find a word in the Word Bank to complete the sentence. Have your child write the word on the line. Then have your child read aloud each sentence and the sentences at the bottom.

Name _____

1. Ted _____ his shoulders.

2. I am _____ a math problem.

3. We were _____ balloons with pins.

4. Were you just _____ your guitar?

5. Andy _____ over the puddle.

6. They _____ to go to the movies.

Grandma was nodding her head and grabbing my hand.
Then she hugged me and patted my head.

Directions Have your child read each word in the Word Bank and circle words with -*ed*
and -*ing* endings, as in *popping* and *shrugged* (not *sing* and *bed*). With your child, read each
sentence. Ask him or her to use one of the circled words in the Word Bank to finish each
sentence and write the word on the line. Then have your child read the sentences at the
bottom and circle words with -*ed* and -*ing* endings.

School + Home

Phonics and Decoding Lesson 25

Name _____

*Example: My soup is <u>hot</u>. Her soup is ___hotter___,
but your soup is the ___hottest___ of all.*

1. Your shoes are not <u>old</u>. I have the _____
   shoes of everyone else in the family.

2. Jim has <u>few</u> cousins. He has _____ cousins
   than Sam has.

3. The light in the hallway is <u>dim</u>. Of all the rooms in
   the house, the _____ is the kitchen.

4. Mario is a <u>quick</u> runner, but I am _____
   than he is in short distances.

5. That was the _____ movie I have ever seen!
   I can't believe you didn't think it was <u>sad</u>.

Mars is a smaller planet
than Jupiter.
Jupiter is the biggest of all
the planets.
A day on Jupiter is shorter
than a day on Earth.

Directions Read the example to your child. For each item, have your child write the *-er* or
-est form of the underlined word in the blank. Remind your child to use *-er* to compare
two things and *-est* to compare three or more things. Remind him or her to double the final
consonant for short vowel words that end with just one consonant as in *dim* and *sad*. Have
your child read the sentences at the bottom and circle each *-er* and *-est* ending.

**School
+ Home**

Phonics and Decoding Lesson 25

More Endings **75**

Name _____

1. face + ed = _____

2. shine + ing = _____

3. prove + ing = _____

4. quote + ed = _____

5. stroke + ing = _____

6. slice + ed = _____

7. change + ing = _____

8. glide + ed = _____

Mom shaded her eyes from the sun.
She was gazing out the window while
Dad was driving.

Directions Today your child learned that when a word ends with a silent *e*, you drop the *e* before you add the endings *-ed* or *-ing* (like *race, raced, racing*). Have your child add the ending indicated in each item to make a new word. Have your child write the new word, use it in a sentence, and then read the sentences at the bottom aloud.

book   _____

pencil   _____

doorway   _____

ceiling   _____

exit   _____

entrance   _____

staircase   _____

elevator   _____

pickle   _____

salad   _____

beverage   _____

dessert   _____

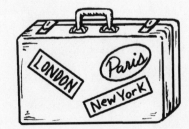

Leo lugged suitcases up the stairs to the guest rooms.
Guests asked desk clerks for restaurant recommendations.

Directions Read each word with your child. Have your child add the ending -*s* to turn each singular word to plural and write the new word on the line. Then have your child read aloud the sentences at the bottom to you and circle any -*s* that has /z/.

Name _____

Word Bank

index	ax	lunch	plus
pass	bunch	latch	stitch
fox	mailbox	dress	walrus
branch	bus	glass	prefix

_____

_____

_____

_____

_____

Fizzy drinks are full of gases.
We make fruit punches from mixes.

School + Home

Directions Have your child read the Word Bank aloud and then circle two words that end in *s*, two that end in *ch* or *tch*, and two that end in *x*. On the lines, have your child write the plural of each circled word using *-es*. Say each new word and take turns using it in a sentence. Finally, have your child read the illustrated sentences aloud.

Phonics and Decoding Lesson 26

Name _____

1. The winners were so proud of (themself).

_____

2. This table comes with five (leaf).

_____

3. A football game has two (half).

_____

4. In spring the cows give birth to (calf).

_____

5. Airport security took away all the (pocketknife).

_____

It was windy down at the wharves.
The busy sailors wore their scarves.

School + Home

Directions Read each sentence aloud and ask your child to write the plural form of the word in parentheses. Help your child change each singular word to its plural form, using *-ves,* and write the new word on the line. Then have your child read the corrected sentence. Finally, read the illustrated sentences together.

Phonics and Decoding Lesson 26

Plurals **79**

Name _____

back	hair	down	star
day	light	tie	line
put	mark	wear	sleep
fall	over	night	pour

1. _____

2. _____

3. _____

4. _____

5. _____

6. _____

The racetrack was next to the fairground.
We had trackside seats at the horserace.

Directions Read each word together with your child. Then help your child create and write six compound words by combining two of the words on each line. When the lines are full, read each compound word together and use it in a sentence. Finally, have your child read the sentences to you.

Phonics and Decoding Lesson 27

blue	**bird**	**seed**
net	**work**	**shop**
note	**book**	**store**
set	**back**	**stroke**
home	**sick**	**bed**

Sherry took shoelaces out of the shoebox.
She laced up her oversized overshoes.

Directions Have your child circle each word in the middle column. Beginning with *blue,* have your child draw a line from each left-column word to the center word. Say the compound word together. Then have your child connect each center word to the word at right and say the new compound word. Repeat for each line of words. Then read the sentences to your child and point to each word part *shoe.*

School + Home

eyeglasses _____ _____

ringleader _____ _____

hummingbird _____ _____

heartwarming _____ _____

everyone _____ _____

jellyfish _____ _____

The headmaster backpedaled to brake the bike.
The firefighters wore waterproof coats.

School + Home **Directions** Help your child read each word. Then ask your child to write the two parts of each compound word on the lines. Help your child use each word—the word parts and the compound word on each line—in a sentence. Read the sentences with your child.

Name _____

sky   *y* to *i* + *es* = _____

belly   *y* to *i* + *es* = _____

navy   *y* to *i* + *es* = _____

hobby   *y* to *i* + *es* = _____

bunny   *y* to *i* + *es* = _____

cranny   *y* to *i* + *es* = _____

bully   *y* to *i* + *es* = _____

flurry   *y* to *i* + *es* = _____

We had no worries about our trip.
We had traveled to different cities and
countries before.

School + Home

Directions Read each singular word with your child. Then ask your child to change the *y* to an *i* and add -*es*, writing the new word on the line. Read each new word and the sentences together.

Name _____

_____ **hurry**

_____ **reply**

_____ **dry**

_____ **fry**

copied _____

carried _____

cried _____

studied _____

Doug and Dave studied.
They copied the spelling lists.
They tried to remember the rules.

Directions For the first four words, have your child change the *y* to *i* and add *-ed* on each line to the left. Then remind your child that a word ending in *-ied* may have come from a base word that ended in *y*. For the last four words, have your child write the base word with *y* on each line to the right. Read the words and have your child use each one in a sentence. Finally, ask your child to read the illustrated sentences to you.

School + Home

Phonics and Decoding Lesson 28

1. Ten _____ jumped in.
One <u>mouse</u> did not.

2. The tree grew one <u>foot</u> each year.
It was forty _____ tall.

3. This flock of _____ is so big,
one more <u>goose</u> would not fit.

4. I looked at all the _____ and
did not know a single <u>person</u>.

5. She was the last <u>woman</u> to join the
baseball team for _____.

6. Except for one bad <u>tooth</u>, his
_____ were very white.

The men fed the oxen.
Children fed corn to the deer and the sheep.

Directions Read each sentence with your child and point out the underlined word. Help him or her write the corresponding plural word on the blank line. Read each completed sentence together. Then read aloud the sentences at the bottom and have your child circle all the plural words.

1. Alicia _____ **seen this.**
(has not)

2. Lim _____ **in this class.**
(is not)

3. Barbara _____ **call back.**
(did not)

4. This jacket _____ **button.**
(does not)

5. _____ **ready to go.**
(I am)

6. The videos _____ **arrived.**
(have not)

"I'm old enough to go there by myself," I said.
"No you aren't, and you can't go!" answered Mom.

Directions Remind your child that a contraction combines two words and has an apostrophe where letters have been taken out. For each sentence, help your child write a contraction from the words in parentheses. Have your child write the new word on the line. Finally, have your child read all the sentences to you.

Name _____

is	**has**
had	**would**

1. What's going on here? _____

2. They'd like to join us. _____

3. We'd met them before. _____

4. He's the tallest in his class. _____

5. Nora's in the car. _____

6. She's got the directions. _____

Larry's studied dancing for three years.
He'd be a great dancer if only he'd practiced.

School + Home

Directions Have your child read each word in the box. Then read the sentences one at a time. Point to the contraction. On the line after each sentence, have your child write the two words that were combined to make the contraction. Work with your child to choose the correct verb from the box. Finally, read aloud the sentences at the bottom, pointing to each contraction.

Name _____

'll (will)	're (are)	've (have)

1. I _____.

2. You _____.

3. He _____.

4. She _____.

5. We _____.

6. They _____.

7. It _____.

You've seen elephants.
They're very big.
I'll stay here while you're feeding them.

Directions Help your child choose letters from the box to form a contraction. Have your child write the contraction on the line. Then work together to write a short sentence using each contraction. Read the sentences at the bottom together.

Phonics and Decoding Lesson 29

Name _____

1. The _____ distance from Earth is very great. (sun, sun's)

2. She did not understand all of the _____ questions. (form's, form)

3. I like to see snow in _____. (November, November's)

4. _____ lakefront is beautiful. (Chicago, Chicago's)

5. My _____ name is Fred. (uncle, uncle's)

6. That _____ has sharp claws. (cat's, cat)

The band's bus broke down.
Huey's brother's best friend was the driver.
The band missed a day's practice.

School + Home

Directions Read each sentence with your child. Then ask your child to choose the best word in parentheses to complete each sentence. Read each completed sentence aloud together. Finally, have your child read the sentences at the bottom.

| s' | es' | 's |

women _____

weight _____

dessert _____

lunch _____

truck _____

monkey _____

pitcher _____

oven _____

geese _____

match _____

fox _____

grandchildren _____

My pet ducks' names are Lucy, Leo, Linda, and Lon. The names' spellings confused my classmates' parents. The ducks ate the people's crackers anyway.

Directions Help your child decide which ending to use to make each word into a plural possessive. Some words are already plural, but most are not. Have your child write the correct ending on each line (*women's, desserts', trucks', pitchers', geese's, foxes', weights', lunches', monkeys', ovens', matches', grandchildren's*). Then read the sentences at the bottom together.

Phonics and Decoding Lesson 30

| Mr. | Dr. | Ave. | D.C. | Jan. | Mon. | Fla. |

212 Dade Avenue _____

Miami, Florida _____

Dear Doctor Dodd: _____

I would like to see you when I visit Washington, District of Columbia, on Monday,

_____

January 11. Mister Lee says you are great.

_____

Last Oct. we bought a pumpkin.
We named it Mr. Squash and displayed
it in the Orange St. store.

Directions On the lines, have your child use abbreviations from the box to rewrite the address and sentence parts. Read the letter aloud together, pointing to the word each abbreviation represents. Then ask your child to read the sentences at the bottom to you.